MY GOOD FRIEND THE RATTLESNAKE

STORIES OF LOSS, TRUTH, AND TRANSFORMATION

MY GOOD FRIEND THE RATTLESNAKE

STORIES OF LOSS, TRUTH, AND TRANSFORMATION

DON JOSE RUIZ

WITH TAMI HUDMAN

PLAIN SIGHT PUBLISHING
AN IMPRINT OF CEDAR FORT, INC.
SPRINGVILLE, UTAH

The opinions and views expressed within this work are the sole responsibility of the author and do not necessarily reflect the opinions or views of Cedar Fort, Inc. Permission for the use of sources, graphics, and photos is also solely the responsibility of the author

ISBN 13: 978-1-4621-1423-8

Published by Plain Sight Publishing, an imprint of Cedar Fort, Inc.
2373 W. 700 S., Springville, UT, 84663
Distributed by Cedar Fort, Inc., www.cedarfort.com

Library of Congress Cataloging-in-Publication Data

Ruiz, Jose, 1978- author.
 My good friend the rattlesnake / don Jose Ruiz.
    pages cm
 Includes bibliographical references and index.
 ISBN 978-1-4621-1423-8 (alk. paper)
 1. Conduct of life. 2. Toltec philosophy--Miscellanea. I. Title.

 BJ1595.R66 2014
 170'.44--dc23

                         2014024976

Cover design by Angela D. Baxter
Cover design © 2014 by Lyle Mortimer
Edited and typeset by Daniel Friend

Printed in the United States of America

10 9 8 7 6 5 4 3 2 1

Printed on acid-free paper

Contents

Foreword

by don Miguel Ruiz

The story of don José's life really begins nine months before his birth. He has no recollection of this part of his life's story, but I do. It all began just before Christmas 1977, when I was in my last year of medical school at the University of Mexico.

My wife and I traveled with our young son, Miguel Jr., to spend the holidays with my parents in San Diego. On Christmas Eve we all gathered at my brother Jaime's house and spent a wonderful evening with my older brothers Luis and Carlos, who were also visiting from Mexico. In the middle of this happy reunion with my family, I experienced a feeling of sadness. It was weird, but for some reason, it felt like this might be the last Christmas of my life.

Coming home to Mexico City, I resumed my studies at the university. The mood there was festive as students looked forward to the end of the year and their upcoming internships. Toward the end of January, there was big celebration in Cuernavaca. I borrowed a car from my brother Luis and drove down with a couple of my friends. It was a great party. We drank a lot that night, had lots of fun, and when the party was over, I made a decision that would change my life. Although my friends and I were intoxicated and tired, we decided to drive back to Mexico City. I drove very fast, wanting to get home before morning. We were laughing and joking, talking about our future as interns, when I was overwhelmed by fatigue. I fell asleep.

I woke up in the hospital the next day. When I asked what happened, the nurse replied, "Don't you remember? You just killed your friends in a car crash!" I was shocked and ashamed, unable to hold back tears. "Sorry," she said quickly, seeing my reaction. "Nothing happened to them. They're alive and well. But," she added, "it's a miracle that the three of you are alive." Apparently, my two friends weren't even in the car at the moment of impact. I was driving, but I was also unharmed. Once I heard that, I began to remember the events of the night before.

I remembered seeing my body asleep at the wheel. I remembered the screams of my friends as they realized they were about to die, and I remembered opening the door and taking them both out of the car before we hit the wall. I remembered all of that, even as I knew my body was asleep in the driver's seat. I remembered embracing my body just before the crash, protecting it from injury. In those days, there were no such things as seat belts or air bags. The car was totally wrecked, and yet we all survived unharmed. It was impossible to know how such a thing could happen; it really was a miracle. I had to ask myself the question, "What am I?" That question sent me on a long journey of discovery away from my life as a medical doctor. Before that night, I had a theory that we are not the body, that we only live within the body—but it was just a theory. Lying in the hospital and remembering the details of the car crash, that theory became a fact, at least for me. My perception completely changed. I had so many more questions, and I needed answers. I wanted the truth.

When I got home from the hospital, my wife was extremely happy. Of course, she was relieved that I was alive and uninjured, but she had also just found out that she was pregnant. The story of my son José Luis began before the holidays the month before. My family's love, my revelations, and the shifts that resulted from the car crash were all part of the process of his creation. The events of the weeks after his conception were registered in my body, my wife's body, and the body of our unborn child.

If we use our imaginations, we can recognize the most

important event of my son's life. It was a race where millions of sperm competed to fertilize an ovum. Only one of several hundred mature eggs was destined to receive the winner, and only one among millions of sperm was destined to achieve its goal. My son Jose was the winner early that December, and his reward was life. A sperm makes up half a cell; the ovum makes the other, and together they create one cell, which divides into countless cells to create a brand–new universe. This universe originates from the merging of two people, and it takes nine months to build. Like all parents, Maria and I created a unique human. There never was a human like him, nor will there ever be. Nine months from conception, a second miracle happened. On September 18, 1978, Jose was born.

My brother Carlos delivered him, and as he placed little Jose into my hands, I was deeply moved. At that moment, I felt as if I was holding myself in my hands. I recognized so much of myself in him. In his eyes I saw a new messenger, someone who would change the lives of countless people with his message of love. There are no words to describe the strong connection I felt to him, a connection that would remain throughout his childhood and that still exists between us today. I have experienced certain moments of Jose's life in my dreams, and in many cases, I've been unable to separate his feelings from my own.

Many events have shaped José and made him the man he is today. He has used all of his precious life experiences to become a true messenger of love, beginning with the events occurring before his birth. In this beautiful book, Jose will tell you many stories about his life and its important lessons.

I have just told you how the story of his life began.

Your Body Is Your Pet

How you treat yourself is how life will respond to you. —Mother Sarita

N ow I would like to introduce to you, my son." I looked around at the sea of people surrounding me, desperately wishing that my older brother had snuck in and was somewhere among them. As I looked around, my heart pounding out of my chest, I reminisced back to just a couple of hours ago. I was sitting comfortably in my living room, playing the latest version of Mario Brothers on my Nintendo when my father invited me to come and watch him speak at the local conference center. When I was a child I would attend my father's workshops where he trained his apprentices on how to have awareness and love in their lives. I noticed at a very young age that my father would randomly call on any of his apprentices to speak in his workshops. You never knew when he was going to put you up in front of everyone to talk, and I knew beyond a shadow of a doubt I wasn't going to avoid this unless I stopped attending his workshops. And that is exactly what I did.

My father had just released his first book, *The Four Agreements*, and was traveling around the United States presenting his teachings to large audiences. I would always find an excuse not to go watch him speak. He was finally speaking at a conference center in our hometown of San Diego, and he asked me to come watch him speak. I came up with whatever excuse I could muster up at the time, and my father asked, "Son, why don't you want to come listen to my lecture? Are you afraid I am going to put you to speak?" I replied, "Yes papa, I am afraid." He said, "Don't worry, son. You are not prepared to speak in front of this type of audience." So I agreed to go with him.

I sat close to the front of the stage and watched as hundreds of people filed in, filling the conference center. I listened attentively to my father's words and watched the people responding to my father with their nods and smiles as well as their laughter and tears. I was feeling so comfortable and enjoying feeling so proud of my father when suddenly I heard these words ring loudly in my ears, "Now I would like to introduce to you, my son." *Oh no*, I thought. *Did I hear right?* I felt my legs begin to weaken and my heart begin to pound. I slowly worked my way to the front of the conference center, looking around, hoping my older brother would magically appear so he could take my place. I walked up the stairs to the stage and stood next to my pops. The crowd was cheering, and my father wrapped his arms around me, gave me a great big hug, handed me the microphone, and sat down.

This is the first time I felt my body as if it were a pet, completely separated from my consciousness. My leg began to shake uncontrollably, and the butterflies in my stomach were fluttering wildly. I could *feel* my nervous system. I quietly scolded my leg, saying *shush, calm down*, just as you would your pet who is being rebellious. I began talking into the microphone and spoke to the audience as well as I could in very broken English. I spoke directly from the heart, knowing that what I was saying probably didn't make much sense to the people I was speaking to. However, what I said at that point didn't really matter. What mattered was that I was experiencing the courage and the mastery of going beyond fear. When you feel your nervous system wake up, that is an indication that it is time to take action. When you are afraid of something or feel that you are in physical danger, you get the natural fight–or–flight response and you take action right away to get yourself out of the situation safely. These were feelings that were developed by humanity back when we were hunters and gatherers and our survival depended on our ability to fight or flee if we were under attack or needed to eat. Now we have different fears to deal with. Sometimes you feel embarrassed, or you are afraid of not being accepted, or maybe you're afraid of losing your job or of saying the wrong thing. In any case, your body has the same fight–or–flight response because those feelings are based on fear. Naturally, we want to use the flight approach, removing ourselves from the situation and finding a safe place to hide. The fight approach would mean facing the problem head on—taking action. It entails finding a way to use your fear as a stepping stone to finding your voice, being more creative, or maybe doing what you really want to do. It may be the next step in your life to over–coming the fear of failure—or the fear of success. Sometimes it is still appropriate to run away and find safety, but in most cases, the fear needs to be faced head on, with an "I am not going to let this fear control me" attitude. With this mind–set, you can take yourself to the next level of fight, which is the fight to becoming your authentic self, to becoming your truth.

Imagine coming upon a large, very wobbly bridge between two cliffs with a river far below. As you approach the bridge, you begin to feel a little nervous about having to cross, but you know you will have to cross if you want to arrive at your destination. You begin to feel the nervous system kick in, and with stomach butterflies and weak knees, you approach the bridge. At the foot of the bridge, you find a small child sitting with his knees up and his face in his hands, crying because he is too afraid to cross. What do you do? You pick the child up, you hold him close to you in your arms, and you carry him across the bridge. At the point of helping someone in need, your nervous system kicks in at a dif–ferent frequency—the frequency of serving another. Why not let yourself be of service to you? Take care of your body. Take care of your pet, and when the nervousness sets in, listen to your emo–tions, pick yourself up, and carry yourself across the bridge. Make the change you need to make to take care of your truth—the change you need to make in order to be yourself.

Once, I was traveling with my father and my grandmother, Mother Sarita. We were in Oaxaca, Mexico, and we came upon the big Catholic cathedral in the center of town. My father said to me, "Son, I want you to go into that church, and I don't want you to come out until you have talked to an angel." I looked at my Grandmother in desperation. She simply nodded and pointed to the front door of the church. I rolled my eyes and with palm to forehead complained, "Oh my God, I am going to be in here forever." I slowly and resistantly walked into the cathedral. I knelt down in front of the altar full of candles and looked up at the beautiful Virgin of Guadalupe, who seemed to be looking down at me with a smirk.

I began praying. "God, please bless me with this, please bless me with that." I was there for what seemed to be forever, when all of a sudden I felt a tap on my shoulder. Slowly, cautiously looking back, I found a beautiful little old lady. I sighed with relief as she said to me, "If you pray, the angel will listen." I smiled courteously and turned back around, having no regard for what the lady had said. I even thought, *What is this crazy old lady talking about?* I shook my head and began praying again. "God, please help me, please hear me, please bring me this, please bring me that." I suddenly had an unusual thought. *If I am praying, then who is listening to my prayer?* Well, I thought, *I* am listening. I am listening to my own prayers. I am the angel. I am the one who has the power to help myself, to take the action to bring to me what I want in my life. *I am* the angel!

With this awareness, I looked up again at the Virgin of Guadalupe. I saw her beautiful face. I saw the symbolism in the points of light, the aura that surrounded her. To me, at that moment, I felt that her aura was a symbol of all the feelings and emotions that are a part of life. This is the way the divine speaks to us, giving us the opportunity to care for ourselves. I then noticed the little angel at her feet, holding her up and supporting her. I saw so clearly that this was a symbol of the mind supporting the human form, supporting the body in all its experiences, feelings, and emotions. If the little angel were to fly away, all of the experiences and feelings would overwhelm her and drop her from her heavenly state. With this support and awareness from our minds, we are able to stalk our thoughts and emotions, care for our bodies, and take action to keep ourselves in a state of heaven wherever life takes us. I thanked the boss and said a little prayer to myself: "May I protect me from myself and find the awareness and love to be of service to myself, my body, and my life."

I ran to the door of the cathedral and searched the gardens with excitement until I found my father and grandmother. I explained to them my findings. "Father, I talked to an angel. *I am* the angel. *I am my own guardian angel.*"

My papa got a huge smile on his face and patted my head with a proud, hair—messing pat. "Good," he said.

HELLO MOONLIGHT

Hello moonlight
this poem
is a leak
from my heart
expressing

the existence of my love
as the blood continues
pumping a message
through my veins to voice it out

hello I'm in love with you
it's a beautiful story
it's my poetry speaking
I'm voicing it out to you

light is illuminating
that dark side
into disintegration
hello I'm in love

inspiration heart
that what you are
unconditional love
is the seed you planted in me

moonlight
in a beautiful night
guides me back home

The Mastery of Complaining

If you say you can't do it, you will not do it. Be aware of what you agree to. —don Miguel Ruiz

I walked out of my bedroom and began to give thanks and say a short prayer at my altar when I felt a very strong burning pain in my foot. I looked down and saw that a scorpion was stinging me. I quickly tossed the innocent creature outside and began looking up remedies on the internet. It wasn't a deadly scorpion sting, obviously, since I am still alive. However, it was going to be very painful and leave a big, blistery sore on my foot. I immediately started to complain about the pain and began to worry about my dog, Yogi. What if it had been him? I gathered up Yogi and went to lie down, for I was beginning to feel a bit woozy. My foot was throbbing with pain and my head was spinning. I closed my eyes and slowly fell into a deep sleep.

I woke up in the dessert and was walking with my grand-mother, Mother Sarita. She was pointing at many large, poisonous scorpions that were crawling all around us. I suddenly became frightened, but she calmed me with her words. "Calm yourself, my son. They do not see us; we are in a dream. In fact, I am not really here, either. I am you bringing you a very important message."

Just as the words came, I looked at the many scorpions surrounding us and found they were stinging themselves with their own tails. They were screaming in pain and slowly dying away. I asked my grandmother, "Why would they do that to themselves? That doesn't make any sense."

Grandmother replied, "This is an old ancient Toltec teaching: when the scorpion stings itself with its own tail, it is like saying, 'I'm not good enough. I am not smart enough or beautiful enough.' You, son, do the same thing every moment that you put attention to your negative self-talk. You sting yourself with your own poison. Be skeptical of your own words and the habit of self-talk that you use to hurt yourself over and over again."

Suddenly I looked down and saw the biggest, most vicious of the scorpions approach me as if it could see me. Its large tail whipped toward me and penetrated me right in the foot. I felt myself falling down, farther and farther, as if I was falling into the depths of Hell. As I was falling I heard my grandmother's voice very faintly, "Heaven doesn't need Heaven, my son. Who needs Heaven is Hell, and you have the ability to take Heaven wherever you go."

I suddenly woke with a start, sweating profusely, reminded of the horrible, agonizing pain in my foot. As I healed from the sting, the pain reminded me regularly to be aware of my negative thoughts toward myself. I noticed that I had mastered something incredibly negative. I like to call it "The Mastery of Complaining." With this awareness, I became skeptical of the talk and took action to change.

My father is a great example of living his life with pure intent and having an incredibly strong will. His heart attack left him with only 16 percent of his heart capacity, which left him in agonizing pain and with very little energy. In fact, when he was being released from the hospital, the doctors told him, "Miguel, you will have to spend the rest of your days just relaxing in your home, attending movies and dinners with very little activity." My father replied, hand behind his back and his fingers crossed, "Yes, doctor."

Once the doctor left, he gathered us around his bed and declared, "There is no way I am going to lie around waiting for the Angel of Death to come for me. I will go out and find the Angel of Death while I continue to do what I love to do." And my father did just that. He continued to travel around the United States and Mexico, teaching his passion to all he came in contact with. He never allowed anyone to see his incredible pain or loss of energy.

I had the opportunity to travel around the world, speaking with my father. On many occasions I would get a little head cold or a stomach flu. My complaints would become incredibly big and very vocal. On other occasions I would feel too tired to speak or exhausted from staying out too late the night before. Again my complaints would be loud and exaggerated. My father always stepped in and took up the slack, even in his weak and painful state. It took a really bad scorpion sting, a dream, and a strong bout of awareness to make me see my selfishness—and how wonderfully I had mastered complaining. I found many excuses and justifications until my awareness was too strong to justify my self-importance. I recognized my father's ability to do the things that inspired him in spite of his physical pains and ailments. I clearly saw my habit of allowing my thoughts and my physical body to take over my life and stifle my passions, creativity, and joy. I am indeed grateful to my father for these teachings, and I continue to work on this awareness on a daily basis.

I am also grateful for the heart that my father was able to accept as a transplant three years ago. After the transplant, the doctor came into his room and asked if he would mind if they studied his heart. They were surprised at his ability to survive, doing what he did, on only 16 percent of his heart capacity. My father, being a medical doctor himself, replied, "Don't waste your time, doctor. It's not in the heart; it's in the will."

THE UNIVERSAL RATTLESNAKE

We are beginning
to feel the truth of our souls
we won't let go

the light in us has shined
let the light keep on shining!

keep feeling, feeling ourselves
to wherever the wind blows
and takes us for a ride
keep on feeling

the universal rattlesnake
celebrates life with us
as it is headed to the sun
it is heading to us
to our sun within
heading to the sun
heading to us!

true love attracts real true love
we are beginning
to feel the truth of our souls
we won't let go!

I be me and you be you
and together let's keep on
shining!!!

keep on shining!!!!!!

children from the sun
that's all we are
we keep on shining!!!!

Take Heaven Wherever You Go

You are a powerful love being; just be aware of your intent.
—Mama Coco

"The world is becoming more and more evil." This is a phrase I hear on many occasions from people I come in contact with. I like to remind them to look back to hundreds of years ago when superstition was so strong, when their barbaric beliefs burned people at the stake and drilled into people's skulls, believing this would release evil spirits. Not to mention the Inquisition and their violent torturing devices. The way I see it, the world is just get—ting more and more aware of and open to the idea that humanity is a whole and that there is no separation. We are all the same, and despite our beliefs or physical differences, we are all part of the same organ of the Earth we call humanity. With this won—derful awareness, the only thing that can come from humanity is peace. Just as we look back and see such barbarism, our children and grandchildren in a few hundred years will look back on this day and age and say, "Look at how barbarically they lived. They believed that something outside of themselves could save them and bring them happiness."

What a beautiful transformation we are participating in! Although it will take time, the world is surely transforming. We all have the opportunity to participate in this change by changing our own world. Instead of taking a picture of a great master and teacher, putting it on our altar, and putting all our faith into this beautiful person and wonderful example, why not take a picture of yourself and place it on your altar, kneel down before your own inspiring being, and put all of your faith into you? This is not showing disrespect to your teacher and master; it is showing the utmost respect and beautiful regard for the teachings of that wonderful master and teacher.

One of my great Toltec teachers is the legend of Quetzalcoatl. In one of my favorite myths, he was a young snake. He went into a hole one day to shade himself from the astonishing rays of the sun. He became comfortable in his little hole and didn't leave for many days. Soon Quetzalcoatl began having thoughts of fear and negativity. The elderly snakes did everything they could to coerce him out of his hiding place, but Quetzalcoatl feared what the world was like out of his comfortable little hole.

"What if they judge me? What if the rays are too bright and I get burned? What if the other snakes don't like me?" He stayed in his hole, and his negative thoughts got so loud and so big that he was paralyzed and afraid to come out.

One day, the most respected of the elders came to Quetzacoatl's hiding place, bringing many of the younger snakes in the village. He sat down right in front of Quetzacoatl's hole. The young snakes were unaware of this as they gathered around the respected elder. He told many stories of the great feathered serpent warriors who fought many battles to overcome fear. They were so brave that they overcame their personal fears, earned their wings, and went back to the sun—their personal heaven, the place where they belonged. He taught the young snakes how to be aware of their thoughts and how to be skeptical of what they were telling themselves. He said, "This is the best way to overcome your fears, to not judge yourself, and to eventually become a feathered serpent warrior and earn the wings that will bring you to your personal heaven." The young snakes listened with big eyes and open hearts. As the elder finished telling his tales, the young snakes ran off with big imaginations of being warriors and fighting great battles against fear.

Quetzalcoatl was also listening deep inside his hole. He heard the words loud—so loud that they were able to stifle out his own thoughts for those brief moments. After the young snakes and the wise elder walked back to the village, the silence became very thick. Quetzalcoatl sat in his hole, contemplating the stories he had just heard. His thoughts returned soon after, and for the first time, he noticed them. He decided to listen to them and to question them with all the courage he could muster. He chose not to believe them and to find the courage to feel, deep in his heart, what he truly was—which, he came to realize, was not his thoughts.

Just then, thunder and lightning began shaking the earth surrounding Quetzalcoatl's hiding place, and the rain began pouring down with a strong force—the force of a mother cleansing herself in order to make a place for beauty to come in with amazing light and love. At first, Quetzalcoatl was frightened of all the rain and the loud thunder, and he tried to hide deeper and deeper in his hole. But his hole was slowly washing away. He started to dig with all his might so that he could continue to shelter himself from the rain when suddenly a ray of light came through the clouds and shone bright upon Quetzalcoatl and what was left of his hiding place. Quetzalcoatl felt the warmth of this beautiful ray and began to see the lies in his fear and negative thoughts about himself. He thought, *This is what I truly am. I am a beautiful light just like this ray. I am not my fears, I am not my thoughts,* I AM. And with this thought, Quetzalcoatl looked at his scales and saw feathers growing in their place. Beautiful wings sprouted on the back of his long, slender body. He turned his face toward the beautiful ray of light and finally noticed no thought at all—just a feeling of peace as he flew himself into his own personal heaven. He flew over Teotihuacan and decided right then that he would build a beautiful pyramid in the Plaza of Hell. He knew that Hell was what truly needed Heaven, and he decided to take Heaven wherever he went.

GIFT

Time is burning
so let's take action
and do our best
and manifest

a gift from the heart
a gift of love

ask a question so the assumption
you've made doesn't make a mess
of your dream
be aware and stop the negativity
from spreading
feel free

don't let it in dreamer
inside your home when it's
knocking at the door
don't let it in

give yourself a gift and break free
from what you imprisoned yourself with
if you believe in you, you will be free
free from the old habits of negativity

it's your dream
you're the artist
messenger of positivity
natural dreamer of love

the time is burning
but the candle its still lit
there is still time to make
a change so
let's be the change

being free from negativity is a beautiful gift
let's change the language we speak to one another
all over the world there is only two
negative and positive which one will you choose to speak?

The Burning Candle

If the candle is still burning, there is still time to change your life, no matter what age you are. —Abuelita Leonarda

"The connection between human life and everything living is *intent*." These were words I heard from my father at the airport in Oaxaca right before we parted ways to fly home after a weeklong spiritual journey. He was flying to San Diego, and I was going home to Malibu. He proceeded to tell me that there is no separation and that my energy will always be connected to his no matter where he is as long as that is my intent. Like a child, I held his hand tight, not wanting to let go. I had such a strange feeling of not knowing if I would see my father again. I gave him a big hug and proceeded to the airplane.

I was sound asleep in my bed in Malibu when I was awakened by the ringing of the telephone at five a.m. It was my grandmother telling me to come to San Diego because my father had just had a heart attack. Trying to remember every little moment, every little word he'd said before I'd left him at the airport in Oaxaca, I jumped in my car and started driving toward San Diego. Everything that I had learned up to that point seemed to be going right out the window just as fast as I was driving to get to my father. When I arrived at the hospital, for the first time in my life, I saw my father very weak, with tubes connected to him everywhere.

I completely lost my composure, and I ran to his side, crying with anguish, "Father, you cannot leave me! Father, this can't be happening."

My father, with all the strength he could muster, sat straight up in bed. With a serious, piercing look, he said, "Is this the way you are going to celebrate the death of your father? No, Son. Get out of this room and fix yourself." Shocked and saddened, I left the room and walked down the hall of the hospital. I began remembering all that I had forgotten—my father's teachings of life and death, of attachment and detachment. I began seeing my selfishness. I was going to take away the last moments of this great man's life with my own selfishness and poison. I was participating in such suffering and such remorse over my father's death, and he wasn't even dead yet. Once I knew that I was again thinking straight, I returned to my father's room, grabbed his hand, and with full intent said, "I am with you now, Pops. I am with you."

My father said, "Welcome back home, my son. Now I want to give you my last teaching.

"You are going to observe suffering like you have never seen before. Your mother, your aunts, and your uncles are going to be in so much pain that they won't know how to express it. They may even say things they don't really mean. But remember, it is not coming from their truth. It is coming from their immense suffering. They are going to make up stories about what I would like from you, about what I would expect from you. But remember, Son, the only thing I want from you is for you to live your life in pure joy and happiness. I want you to do what you love to do and to always be in love with life. Do you understand what I'm telling you, Son?"

I replied, "Yes, Father," and he said right back, "Okay, good. Now get out of the room. I have many others I need to talk to before I go."

That was the last time I spoke to my father before he went into a nine-week coma. Everything he had predicted began happening. Everyone was crying and sad, but I was doing as my father suggested. I was joking around, attempting to bring some joy into the household, telling funny stories and memories of my father that brought me happiness. My elders began telling me many things that my father would wish from me: "Jose, your father would want you to do this; your father suggested that you do that." I even got a very emotional, "Jose, it is all your fault that your father is in this condition," and a, "What's wrong with you, Jose? Why are you so happy? You need therapy!" With those comments, I began to feel some anger, but I remembered what my father had told me in the hospital room. I was thankful at that time for my father's message. Otherwise I might have taken what I heard personally and been hurt by their words. But I knew they were just speaking out of hurt and suffering. I quickly removed myself from the situation and went to my room.

There I found an amazing gift my father had given me when I was sixteen years old. He had walked into my room so proudly with the beautifully wrapped package. It was about the size of the new Nintendo game that had just came out that year, and, thinking that's what it was, I quickly unwrapped it. I didn't find the new Nintendo game, but I found a picture of my father with a very serious look. He said to me, "This gift is for you to know that when you do something rebellious or something you are not proud of, I do not have to know about it. When you look at this picture of me, you will know enough."

Believe it or not, it totally worked! Each time I came home from a wild night out with my friends, I would see his face staring at me with that endearing yet powerful look, and I would liter—ally have to turn the whole picture around. Even my friends who came home with me would look at the photo and say, "Geesh, Jose, your father is staring at me," and they would also turn it around.

However, in my moment of anguish over my father's heart attack and trying to keep my composure through all of the drama and emotional pain going on in my home, I saw this photograph in a completely different way. I saw my father looking back at me with my own eyes. I realized the power of the gift he had given me. It was the power to look at myself with my own knowing eyes and be able to see my truth.

At that moment, I saw my father's divinity and his eternal—ness, and I saw clearly how I could contribute to keep him and his divine message alive. I looked into my father's eyes, and with full intent made the decision to continue to teach my family's message throughout the world. I found the old books and audiotapes he had made of what he called "Angel Training," and I began to study his words. I realized that he was teaching it in small baby steps, and I decided that in order to get the message out, I needed to teach it in one full course. No more levels—just the teachings as a whole. Those who are going to get it will get it, and those that don't, won't. And I began to teach.

After nine weeks, my father woke up from his coma. He had to learn many things over again—how to walk, how to speak. He even had to remember the faces of his loved ones. But once he was feeling better, he asked me one day, "Jose, what have you been up to?" I told him about the classes I had been teaching, about how I was teaching Angel Training in a totally different way. With pure interest and excitement, my father asked to see what I was doing. He came to one of my workshops. He saw that I was sharing the entire message. No A–B–C or 1–2–3 anymore. He was also surprised to find that the participants seemed to be getting it. They were taking the entire message and using it to change their lives. He became excited and eager to start sharing the message again, and with much happiness I was blessed to again teach alongside my father.

Over those few months, I saw so many things that my father had taught me over the years. I saw the addiction to suffering that was rampant in me and those surrounding me. I saw how this parasite is a real, living being, and when there is something to suffer over, this being comes out in full force, attempting to make himself as real and eternal as we are in our truth. If we allow ourselves to suffer, it takes its chance to have power over us, feeding us with lies and making us feel mortal so that it can feel immortal. I saw so clearly how I would go in and out of truth and lies. But when the lies would start to take over, I would hear my father's words ring loudly in my ears: "Once you wake up, Son, you can't go back to sleep." And I was fully awake.

I could see the beauty of forgiveness. Not only forgiving those around me that may have said or done something to hurt me through their own suffering, but the beauty of forgiving myself. Forgiving myself for everything and knowing that I am who I am today and that nothing in my past can change that. It may have brought me to this point, but change can only happen right here and right now. Forgiving humanity as a whole, not only for past mistakes but for mistakes made now and even in the future. Knowing that all humans have the same characteristics and that there will always be suffering, mistakes, and pain, so why not forgive? Why not forgive everything now?

This leads me to one of the most important teachings: you don't have time! You don't have time to suffer, you don't have time to wallow in sadness, and you don't have time to be a victim. You don't have time. Spend your time enjoying life, having beautiful memories of those who have passed on, and forgiving and for-getting those who have hurt you. Why continue to give a person who hurt you power over your life? Whether that person hurt you a long time ago, yesterday, today, or even in the future, find a way to forgive them. You don't have time. Time is of the essence, so why not make your time a living, growing, peaceful heaven? This, in my opinion, is the only advantage of time and the only reason we live in a place where there *is* space and time—so we can learn how to utilize it wisely and for our loving benefit. Now, with this new awareness, you have time, so make it beautiful.

A WALK IN NATURE

A rabbit is hiding inside
a magicians hat
when it's pulled out
it's cheered by the crowds

time to wake up
and stop the cruelty we do
to animals and ourselves
let's change the program

and live once again
in a dream of respect
the organic love of nature
let the rabbit free

it's time to wake up
from the negative dream we fear
set ourselves free
and stay free

not hide in that hole
of darkness inside
the ground anymore
just listen to yourself

it's time to feel the sun
and dream in love

we are the artist
that is born to create

with all of my love
dreaming with you
is heaven on earth
nurturing to my soul

we know our soul is home
just listen to yourself and . . .

run free, rabbit
run, run free
and run with me
we are only dreams

and we are free
with passionate expression
we can do anything
we are only dreams

on our way back home
an authentic light from the sun
it shines wherever it goes
and then you know everywhere is home

and that is nature to my soul
we all heading to the same place
where everywhere we go is home
would you like to keep walking with me?

We all are walking to the same place, together!!!

Attention, Intention, Action

Wherever you put your attention, life happens. —Barbara Emrys

Attention is the key to opening your heart. When I was seventeen, I was in India. One of the most memorable experiences I have ever had happened in the plaza at the center of the city of Shirdi. There was a swami doing a special ceremony that was intended to open a vortex. As I watched in amazement and wonder, I noticed the people surrounding the master who, with pure intent, were absorbing his powerful energy. With their attention on him and their arms in the air, they were opening their hearts to his teachings and words. With their intention and will to see this master step into the unknown, they were able to witness the opening of a vortex. I also noticed one gentleman standing in the circle, watching with arms closed across his chest, attempting to watch but seeming too afraid to let go and open his heart.

When the ceremony was finished, everyone spoke with excitement about their experience and told how they were able to see and feel the power of the master and the opening of the vortex. When it came time for the closed gentleman to speak, he said, "I did not see or feel anything." When I was in the plaza observing this teaching, I had no idea at the time of the implications this blink of a memory would have on me. Because this person was closed to the idea of opening a vortex, he was unable to see what the others with open hearts were seeing. When you are able to put your attention on something with full intent, things start to shift. Just as in the old Shaman tradition, you shift your assemblage point. Attention is just the first step.

Attention is the target and how you see that target. You see the target with your eyes and then feed it into your brain, which is where the intent begins to take form. When you pick up the bow and arrow and begin shooting the target, this is the intention, this is your will. You may be missing the target, but you are giving life to the bow and arrow. Your intention and will is to hit the bull's–eye, and practice is the action. You practice and practice shooting the bow and arrow until you begin hitting the bull's–eye. You practice your form and your precision in order to manifest your will or intent to hit the target. The action you take brings forth your will or intent and makes it a reality.

My father told me a story many years ago written by the poet Homer. He said that the Greek Gods were in the heavens speak–ing to one another. One of them said, "We only exist because the humans believe in us. When the humans stop believing in us, we will no longer exist." Putting your attention on something is the birth of that thought, idea, or dream. Once you intend to bring that thought into reality, that is the time to take action. Nurture the idea to make it grow into its full potential.

Look at your life as a blank canvas. The world is full of ideas that flow through you at all times. You decide what ideas you want to give your attention to. What you see with full attention you bring into your brain, which is your art studio. This art studio is where you will begin to create your life, your own heaven, your masterpiece of art. This is where you will manifest your intention. Your decisions paint the canvas. Only you can bring forth an idea or a dream. There is nothing stopping you from creating what you want in your life. There aren't really any rules, and your own art studio is your playground. It's time to start playing. The brushes and tools you use in your art studio are your words. Words are very powerful. Listen to what you are telling yourself. Does it allow things to happen for you, or does it uninspire you and put a stop to the action you are taking to fulfill your dreams? Stalk your own thoughts and words, and know that you can change them at any moment. You can paint, draw, or mold them into whatever inspires you.

When I was a little boy around eleven years old, I had a strong desire to see a jaguar. I was visiting the Mayan Jungles with my father, and I kept begging him, "Papa, I want to see a jaguar, I want to see a jaguar." I repeated this request over and over again, giving full attention to my desire. After hearing my request multiple times, my father turned to me abruptly and with power in his words, said, "If you really want to see a jaguar, Son, then you will see a jaguar." And he turned and walked away from me. There came the intent. I continued to explore the jungle–filled ruins in Palenque. Taking action, I searched with the words of my father repeating over and over in my mind: "You will see a jaguar." Then, suddenly, I saw some eyes looking at me through the thick trees and plants. The eyes were bright blue, and they watched me with curiosity. We locked eyes for only a moment before the creature turned and flamboyantly flipped its tail toward me, walking into the thick jungle. I saw its golden fur covered in dark spots and knew that I had just seen a young jaguar. Knowing that the mother couldn't be too far away, I felt a little frightened, and I ran as fast as I could back to the hotel to tell my father what I had experienced.

This world is multidimensional. What we put our attention on is what we are going to perceive. I could have walked all over that jungle and not even noticed that small jaguar looking at me through those plants, but because I was looking for it and my intent was strong, the action I took toward my intent brought me to my desire.

I used to think of a dream catcher as something mystical and outside of me that would create my dreams for me. Then I realized that *I* am the dream catcher, and if I pay attention, with full intent, I have the power to choose what dream I am going to catch next.

RIVER OF POSITIVITY

Return to positivity
with gratitude to negativity
for letting us know what to change
for letting us know what we don't want
for reflecting how we are eating our own poison

lady awareness
thank you for introducing me
to the story teller that tells me my story
to put my attention to what the river took away

I will let life be thy witness
like an out-of-body experience
but not like in sleeping dream
but in awakened state of lucid dream

letting the waterfall flow
in what force she feels like
she free and we feel her within us
life throws us into the river to swim in her

looking into our honest eyes
smokey mirror is getting cleared
the spirit can be felt in everything
especially in the space between words

so let us close our eyes
and dream a beautiful
and then open them
and look what the river
is bringing today

My Good Friend
the Rattlesnake

Once my stepson and his two friends were talking about what they were going to do when they graduated from high school. My stepson asked the other two young men, "How would you guys like to be remembered?" One replied, "I would like to be remembered by how much money I made and how successful I am." The other responded, "I want to be remembered by how talented of a musician I am." My stepson, Kason Hudman, responded, "I want to be remembered by how well I treated others."
—don Jose Ruiz

Living in the mountains of San Diego, during the spring and summer months I get the opportunity to see a few rattlesnakes enjoying life on my property. The rattlesnake has been a great teacher to me in my life experience. When a rattlesnake is young, it is very dangerous because it cannot control its poison. If it were to bite you, it would release all of its poison into you, and it could potentially be fatal. Once a rattlesnake grows and becomes an adult, it learns to control its poison. If it were to bite you, it would only release a small amount of poison. This makes your chances of survival much greater. As young humans, we are inexperienced and unaware. Much like young rattlesnakes, when we react to others, we tend to release all our poison. This not only hurts those around us but hurts us as well. However, because we are young, we continue to learn with each reaction. As we grow up and get older, we gain life experience and wisdom. In a healthy situation, we learn to communicate effectively and assertively, using wisdom and respect to control how much poison we bring to our relationships. With age and awareness, we begin choosing our battles, and we become slow to feed most dramas that come into our lives. If we have had unhealthy relationships growing up or have experienced trauma or some type of abuse, we may still learn to control our poison, but we may choose, without awareness, to use it in a negative way—perhaps to manipulate or control others. This type of poison can cause great suffering and confusion in relationships. With awareness and practice, we can learn to control ourselves and the poisons we bestow upon those we say we love the most.

Many humans are addicted to suffering. We latch onto it because we have been taught that to be human means to suffer. It is where we feel comfortable. When I was a young teenager, I would attend my father's Toltec apprenticeship classes. He would have several apprentices sitting in a circle. They passed around a large stick with eagle feathers attached to the top of it. The person with the stick would get the chance to talk. As a young boy, I noticed that when someone would get the stick, they would tell stories of great suffering. In my perception it seemed that they were competing with each other: Who was suffering the most? When I got the stick, I didn't have any sad stories to tell. I came to the conclusion that being an adult meant having great suffering and sad stories to tell. So with that belief, I decided that the next time I attended one of my father's classes, I would have a story of suffering to tell. Off I went on a quest to find suffering and become an adult. I found my first crush and, soon after, my first heartbreak.

Once I began searching for suffering, it came to me in leaps and bounds. Throughout my teenage years the suffering continued. I was spreading poison without any awareness. It was all brought on by myself. I began hanging around with gangs and started using heavy drugs. I was going against myself as well as against my parents until, one weekend, it was my weekend to stay with my father in San Diego. I was seventeen at the time, and I was very resistant to go. My friends were going to the beach to party for the weekend, and I really wanted to join them. My father would not take no for an answer, and I reluctantly went with him to his home in San Diego. When I returned to Tijuana the next Monday morning, I got some really disturbing news. One of my best friends had been killed in a car accident on the way to the beach. I was in mourning over my friend, overwhelmed with emotions ranging from guilt and anger to relief and gratitude. I was thankful that I hadn't been in that car, yet immensely guilty that it had happened to him and not me. I came to the realization that I needed to change my life. I went to my father and disclosed to him the destructive way I had been living, and with tears fall—ing down his cheeks, he said, "Welcome back home, my son. Welcome back home."

At that point in my life, I began to see a pattern of attach—ment—my attachment to my home in Tijuana, my friends, my drug contacts, and my crazy lifestyle. I could see the attachment I had to past love relationships and my attachment to my uncon—trolled poison, but most of all my attachment to suffering.

As humans, we have moments when we recognize our insan—ity and want to make a change, so we make a beautiful love offer—ing to the Angel of Death. We remove the destructive mask we are wearing. The mask of lies and attachment that has felt so comfortable for so long that we say, "Thank you for the good times and thank you for the bad times." We give it to the Angel of Death as an offering of gratitude. Then, a few days later, we begin to feel uncomfortable. The feeling becomes so strong that we find ourselves running back to the Angel of Death's door and knock—ing with desperation. "Can I have my mask back?"

It seems to be a process we go through when we are trying to release a painful habit. We go to the refrigerator and take out all the spoiled food we can find. We begin to make a lovely dish of spoiled goulash, and we serve ourselves up a big plateful. We sit down and eat the entire plate of food and go to bed. In the middle of the night we awake with a very intense stomach ache.

The tummy pain doesn't seem to subside, so the next morning we go to the doctor and tell him about the horrible stomach pain. He sends us home with some antacids and we feel a little better, but we go to the refrigerator and serve ourselves up another big plate of rotten food. The scenario happens all over again. We wake up in the middle of the night with horrible stomach pain, and we go to the doctor the next day and say, "I don't understand why this keeps happening to me!" While the doctor is listening and trying to figure out what might be causing this intense pain, we pull out a baggie of the leftover rotten food and start eating it again.

To understand why it is so difficult to release ourselves from our old habits, especially the painful ones, we must look closely at our lives and find out what rotten food we are attached to.

My grandmother used to teach that life is about learning to detach. She would say, "Attachment and detachment are so easy. It's as easy as taking a breath. You breathe in . . . attach. You breathe out . . . detach. If you were to breathe in and hold it, you would suffocate. Living life to its fullest is about letting go—the detachment." As a great Buddhist master said, "Life is measured by how well we live, how well we love, and how well we learn to let go."

Which brings me back to my friend the rattlesnake. Every so often, the rattlesnake sheds its skin. Can you imagine if every time the rattlesnake shed its skin it held onto it, attaching to it and carrying it everywhere it went? That is what we tend to do as humans. We take our old experiences, good and bad, and we drag them with us everywhere we go. Imagine if we were to detach and start fresh with each new relationship, with each new day. What a beautiful offering of love to yourself and everyone you come in contact with! The past is not real anymore if we can practice focusing on the moment where all change takes place. Letting go of old habits and detaching from old ways of living can be a difficult task. Only you can deprive yourself of the change and the peace that comes from it. You can bring back all those old habits and begin to wear that old mask again, but with awareness and patience as well as practice, those old habits will begin to change. Your practice of detachment will become easier, and letting go will become as easy as taking a breath.

UNCONDITIONAL LOVE IN ACTION

Heaven on earth is possible
when your love takes the action
heaven on earth is possible
it's a gift of inheritance

freedom from
living in unawareness
free from ourselves
free from myself

today I start to change the world
by changing my world
if you do it too then we'll do it together
an act of love is a gift of humbleness

I believe we can make a difference
riding the train of positivity
destination is wherever life takes us
and there is where our message goes

as the gardener plants the seeds
and knows what is being planted
ask yourself what you are planting
no one needs to know it's a surprise as it grows

today I start to change the world
by changing my world
and if you do it too we'll change it together
an act of love is a gift of generosity

with our impeccable word in action
our world, inside and out

the dream we dream together
will change
let's take our inheritance

and restore our culture
our human culture
the messengers of a new
generation are returning home

we are all in the same tribe
humanity's unconditional love!!!

The Illusion of Judgment

Sometimes you have to get comfortable in the uncomfortable until the uncomfortable passes and you are comfortable again.
—My grandfather, don Jose Luis Ruiz

Imagine a beautiful little bird sitting up in a tree, singing away. It's chirping and tweeting the most beautiful song you have ever heard. Now imagine that the same little bird decides that he can't sing because he is too afraid of what the other birds will think. They might make fun of him or not like what he is singing. Doesn't this sound ridiculous? Birds and most non−domesticated animals are great examples of living a carefree life, doing what they love to do, and just enjoying each moment of life. They aren't worried about what the other birds or animals think. They just do what feels good in the moment.

I enjoy being judged because it is a good test for me. It is, of course, a time of great discomfort! But when I feel this type of discomfort, I tend to pause for a moment, take a deep breath, and get as comfortable as I can in the discomfort. This pause brings me to an awareness of my possible reactions to this discomfort and judgment. Instead of automatically reacting to the criticism and wanting to be accepted by those who are judging me, I am able to take a look at what I am doing and who I am being. I ask myself, "Are these actions making me truly happy? Are they bringing me closer to who I truly am?" With this newfound awareness, I am able to decide whether or not I am being who I want to be despite any judgments or outside opinions. In fact, it is usually the times when I am getting closer and closer to my truth that I get the most judgments and opinions. These judgments and opinions not only come from outside sources but also from the parasites of doubt and fear within my own mind. So with that, I can come to the conclusion that being judged usually means I am on the right path to my authentic self.

Just like the little bird singing his heart out, I am usually on the path of living my own passion when the most judgments come in. Being skeptical of all judgments and opinions, whether they are from an outside source or from your own thoughts, is the best way to filter through those thoughts and opinions and choose to listen only to those that are serving your truth and allowing you to become your authentic self.

After my best friend was killed in a car accident, I went to my father and told him about the negative life I was living. I told him about the drugs and gangs I had been involved in, and I asked him for help. He sent me to India to stay with my stepmother, Gaya, and to study with a swami named Kaleshwar and my stepbrother Rama Krishna.

When I arrived, I was feeling homesick and desperate to go back to my old life, the life I was comfortable in even though it was destructive and unhealthy. I walked to the center of the town of Shirdi and sat in the plaza where there were a few benches and a beautiful fountain. I enjoyed sitting on the benches in the plaza and studying the Indian culture, which I wasn't quite used to yet. As I was calculating a plot to get myself back to Mexico and my friends and family, a couple of English-speaking businessmen walked up and stood next to the bench I was sitting on. They were talking about business using terms and big words I had never really heard before. I was doing my best to understand them and enjoying listening to their English, wondering what the big words meant, when a beautiful old man came into the center of the plaza. He was a vagabond that I had seen wandering the city on a couple of other occasions. He began dancing and singing vajhans very loudly while moving around the fountain, completely unaware or unconcerned that anyone was watching him.

He was dancing and singing for what seemed to be a couple of minutes when one of the businessmen said, "Look at that old man. I think he is crazy."

The other man listened intently with his hand on his chin. He sat in silence for a few moments, watching the old man with amazement and wonder before he replied, "That man might be crazy, but he is happily in love with life." Then he turned to his colleague and asked, "Are you happily in love with life?"

His colleague thought for a moment and then said reluctantly, "No."

"Then who is crazy?" was his companion's reply.

The wise words of this clean−cut, well−dressed stranger penetrated deep within my heart. I thought to myself, *Am I happily in love with life? Am I truly doing what I love to do?* At that point in my life, I had numbed myself completely with drugs and alcohol. I didn't even know who I was beyond the immense craving for my next high and the intense excitement of how I was going to score it. Not to mention the strong, fearful paranoia of getting caught and incarcerated. I thought to myself, *I don't even know who I am.*

I jumped up from the bench, and with my hand over my heart, I bowed deeply toward the gentleman who seemed to speak directly to me. Then, with pure love, I bowed toward the beautiful vagabond who was still dancing and singing, oblivious to me and my gracious bow. When we are in our passion, doing what brings us joy with an open heart, full of love for self and life, the judgments of others can't really touch us. We don't allow them to, and even more important, we don't believe them. It is just like the story of Siddhartha when he was sitting under the Bodhi Tree. He was getting arrows thrown at him left and right, but before they could even penetrate him, he was turning them into roses. If you don't judge yourself, no one else can judge you, and the judgments will die in your mind.

After the epiphany I had in the plaza of Shirdi, I went into a rebellious funk. I was very skeptical of what I was being taught. I didn't really know who I was, and that thought made me feel even more angry and rebellious. At that time I really enjoyed eating meat, and the swami taught the benefits of eating vegetarian. So with a rebellious heart, I skipped class one day and went into town to get a pizza filled with pepperoni and sausage. As I was ordering the pizza, a voice came into my head, saying, "Go to the temple." I dismissed the voice as I placed my order and sat down at a table to wait for my pizza. As I was waiting, the voice came into my head even louder: "Go to the temple." Luckily, my pizza arrived at about the same time, so I dismissed the voice again. I got myself a large slice of pizza. My mouth watered with excitement. I took a big bite of the gooey, cheesy, meaty pizza. As I bit into it, the taste was not what I was expecting. It was not as good as it looked. In fact, it tasted terrible. But with disbelief, I took another big bite. With the second bite came a very loud call, "Go to the temple." The pizza tasted so bad and the voice was so strong that I decided I needed to listen. I left the pizza and ran all the way to the temple.

When I arrived, there was a very long line to get in. I decided that I would ignore the voice and go back into town to find something else to eat. As I began walking away, the old temple groundskeeper grabbed my arm and said, "We have been waiting for you to arrive. Come." He took my hand and lead me to the front of the line and stood me in front of the big marble statue of Sai Baba to pray. As I knelt there, I could feel the presence of the people as they approached the statue, graciously praying with open hearts and putting all of their faith into this magnificent replica of an amazing teacher and master. I felt a strong, loving energy that I hadn't felt in a long time. I could feel their opulent faith as they each said a little prayer. I couldn't understand the language, but it was beautiful and full of love. I remembered my grandmother Sarita and felt the familiar presence of her loving faith and teach-ings. I thought of the moment when my father had sent me to pray in the church in Oaxaca, Mexico, and instructed me not to leave until I had talked to an angel. I remembered that when I prayed, I was the one listening and that with my own power and choice,

I, and only I, could answer my prayers. If I put all my faith into myself, in the manner demonstrated by these loving and faithful people, I could create whatever life I chose. I began remembering my father's teachings, the Toltec lineage I was born into, and the positive message of responsibility and power that it teaches. I had a small glimpse of what I truly was, and I knew that it was pure love. I had gotten lost in an immense desert of fear. I knew in that moment the gift my father had given me in sending me to India.

I left the temple with a tear running down my cheek. The line of people was gone, and the temple was empty. My stepbrother Rama Krishna was sitting outside with open arms and a warm hug. He knew without any words what I had experienced. He took my hand, and we walked together, silent, hand in hand to the cafeteria, where we enjoyed a delicious vegetarian meal together.

The week before I left India, my stepmother, Gaya, asked Swami Kaleshwar if he would give me an Indian name before I left. Swami seemed to be very reluctant. He said, "You want me to give a name to the kid who would skip out on class and go into town to eat meat?" Mama Gaya just smiled and said, "Of course, only as you wish, Master Swami." The day before I left, we went to the river, and the swami had us meditate there all day. As I was bathing and meditating in the river, I gave silent thanks to India for all the eye-opening and life-changing moments. I thanked my father, Mama Gaya, and my stepbrother for their love, kindness, and patience. I thanked Swami Kaleshwar for all his positive teachings and his love.

That evening, as we sat together around the table to eat my last meal in the Ashram, Swami Kaleshwar called me to his seat at the head of the table. He asked if I had enjoyed my stay in India. I said, "Oh yes, Master. I enjoyed it very much. I am even wearing an 'I love India' T-shirt."

As I jokingly opened my jacket to reveal the T-shirt I was wearing, he laughed and asked, "Would you like to leave here with a spiritual name?"

I said, "As you wish, Master. I am just grateful for all the teachings and love you have bestowed upon me."

He stood up and said, "With great honor, I would like to

give you the name of Kaleshwar. I know you are not of this lin-
eage, but I would like you to take my name and, with respect and
honor, go back to your lineage of truth and teach not only your
own message but also the message of truth that you have learned
here."

With my hand over my heart, I bowed to my Indian master
with deep gratitude, and with great appreciation, I thanked him
for the beautiful gift.

As I was returning to my seat, the opinions from some of the
students in the Ashram came pouring in.

"Hey, Swami, how could you give him your name? He doesn't
come to class, and I saw him yesterday in town eating chicken."

"Yeah, Swami. He doesn't even practice the true Hindu
teachings or do his chores in the Ashram."

Swami quickly put his hand up to stop the judgments. As the
roar of the commotion quieted down, he said, "He may not practice the teachings completely, but he does what he likes to do. He
doesn't follow anyone just to be part of the group. He is skeptical
of what people tell him, and he chooses only the teachings that
serve him in his own beliefs and individuality. These are the traits
that make a true master, that is why he is worthy of my name."

I bowed deeply again toward Swami and cautiously took my
seat. Although the judgments from the other students felt like
sharp arrows piercing my heart, I noticed that the humble love I
felt for all the teachings I had received and for the Indian culture
I had learned from was bigger and deeper than the pain of those
arrows. I felt a strong sense of loyalty toward the beautiful Hindu
teachings, as well as a loyalty toward the teachings of my Toltec
upbringing. I knew then that when I returned to Mexico the next
day I would take what I had learned and share it in many different
ways throughout my life.

Not being accepted by others and being judged for who you
truly are is one of the greatest fears of the human condition. This
is why so many people go to their deathbed with their song, or
their painting, or their great invention still inside of them, tucked
away deep in their heart where it is safe. When you are putting your truth out there with full passion and great vulnerability,

turning those arrows into roses becomes crucial. Remember, with each judgment, the path of truth you are on and the joy and peace you feel as you remain true to your path. When that fear of rejection bubbles up, remember that the judgment itself is also coming from fear. With this awareness, you can use empathy for the one judging you to allow your love to open up so big that it not only stifles out your fear but also reflects to the judger his own fear and his own love. As you become skeptical of everything you allow into your life, listening with full attention to all you have attracted, you can truly learn the art of non–judgment not only toward others but, most importantly, toward yourself. Once the judgments die in your own mind, it is impossible for anyone else to judge you.

WORKING IN THE GARDEN OF LOVE

A seed is planted
in the soil ground
and the mother waters it
with her element in rain

and the rays of love
feed it with the fire within
that burning element
it's an art, the letting go

dancing in the sky
everything is divine
let us fly to the sun and come back
as beautiful mother nature's love

we feed our plant
we feed our creation
working in the garden of love
our garden, our home

we take the action
positive planting
grow with positive love
you are love
they are love
we are love
I am love
knowing deep inside
we are all love

we are the plant of change
and there will be fruit to give
working in the garden of love
serving mother nature's dream

Everything Is Spiritual

Nobody can tell you that what you're doing is not spiritual. With common sense, we know that everything we do in life is spiritual because we are spirit in action. —A thought I had in Shirdi, India

As I sat watching the Tibetan Bowl Master carefully place her beautiful bowls strategically around the mat, I felt a sense of excitement and peace for what I was about to experience. I lay down on the mat and got myself all cozy with pillows under my head and comfortable cushions surrounding my body. The Master placed a beautiful soft blanket over me to keep me warm. I closed my eyes and brought myself into a fully relaxed state. I wanted to be able to completely enjoy the healing and cleansing she was about to perform.

The Master said a few words in Sanskrit and began tapping all the bowls around me, making a beautiful, amazing vibration. I could feel my body vibrating. The sounds resonated from the top of my head all the way down to my toes. I relaxed completely, and my mind cleared as I focused on the subtle vibrations in my body. My body was completely still, but the vibrations were deep and penetrating. As she tapped the bowls, she repeated a beautiful mantra of OOOOOMMMMM. She repeated it over and over again, and it brought such a peace and wonder to me. I knew that there was something bigger, beyond my physical body. This beautiful ritual of repetition brought to mind one of my favorite tunes and the memory of being in one of the most amazing concerts I had ever attended. I realized at that moment that my experience in the concert was not much different from what I was experiencing at that very moment.

The Master continued her ceremony, tapping and chanting for more than forty-five minutes. It felt amazing and relaxing, exciting and penetrating. When she was finished, she gently cradled my head in her hands and placed her thumbs on my forehead, touching the spot between my eyebrows.

I slowly opened my eyes, making contact with her sparkling eyes and her smile shining wide and beautiful down upon me. She saw me looking up at her and asked, "So how did you like it?"

I was so grateful. I replied, "Oh, I loved it so much. It reminded me of an Ozzy Osbourne concert." Her expression changed into a look of surprise and confusion. I quickly began to explain myself. "I don't mean any disrespect. It was the most beautiful experience. One time when I was at an Ozzy Osbourne concert, Ozzy began singing a song called 'Mama I'm Coming Home.' I began singing the words along with the crowd, and as the lyrics, 'Mama I'm coming ho OM OMe, I'm coming ho OM OMe' repeated over and over again, I looked all around the stadium, and there I was with sixty thousand metalheads om-ing. I closed my eyes in that moment and felt a peaceful vibration from the tips of my toes all the way through the top of my head, the very same peaceful vibration I felt here as you performed your beautiful healing." The Master was satisfied with my story, and I could feel her acceptance of and love for my spiritual experience. She told me that there are many aspects of spirituality and that not one of them is wrong. They are just different. In that moment I realized that finding something that inspires you or brings you into a spiritual state has nothing to do with what is going on outside of you.

Everything is spiritual. Anything that touches you or makes you feel a connection with life brings a spiritual aspect with it, and the wonderful thing is that everyone is different. There are so many different ways to worship. There are so many ways to feel inspired and connected. The place I feel the most spiritual is in a rock concert. I can close my eyes, and the music and the wave of the audience make an intense vibration. It is the same vibration you feel when you are praying, chanting, or meditating. It is that subtle hum deep down inside, the hum of God or the Source or a higher power. It is that subtle reminder of truth we can all feel if we are able, one way or another, to empty the chatter in our mind. There are many different ways to find that hum or that peaceful silence. It is usually found in a place where you become fully present in the moment, and it brings you to a place where you loose track of time and space.

A friend of mine once asked me to take him to my favorite meditation place. That night I happened to be going to an Iron Maiden concert, so I took him along. He could not understand how I could meditate under such circumstances. I just closed my eyes and felt the vibration of the music and the energy of the sta—dium full of Iron Maiden fans. My friend stood and watched me, perplexed. He could not feel the peace I was feeling. In fact, he left after just a few songs. He wasn't wrong, nor was I; we were just different in our perception of what brings a feeling of inner peace and light. There is no right or wrong way to meditate, and there is no right or wrong way to find your own inner peace, your spirituality. Everything is spiritual in its own unique way.

There is a big war surrounding spirituality. It is the war of belief. The thought is that "my God is better than your God, and if I don't teach you everything there is to know about my God and you don't accept it, you will not be 'saved.'" Acceptance is the key. None of us really know for certain which religion or spiritual practice is right or true. If you take away the dogma, it boils down to each belief being exactly the same: a place of love, respect, and acceptance for all life in every form. In each form of prac—tice, we are taught not to judge, but the dogma prevents us from fully accepting others and what they believe to be truth for them. This inability to allow others to believe what they choose without trying to change them and forcing what we think is true upon them creates a tension among humanity. This tension causes war, which has shown in the past to be a road to rampant destruction. Allowance and acceptance brings a pure, nonjudgmental aspect to your life. If you can allow someone to just *be*—be the person they choose whether you agree with them or not—you will bring pure respect to and avoid judgment in your own being.

After I returned home from India, I went to Tijuana to see all my old friends. They had planned a big party for my return. In my old neighborhood, they used any excuse to throw a party. A few hours into the party, a close friend of mine became very drunk. He came to me and said, "Jose, show us something. Your grandmother is a curandera, your father is a nagual, and you just returned from studying with a swami in India. Come on, show us something magical!"

Of course, I said, "Come on, dude, let's just have a good time." But, being drunk, he wouldn't take no for an answer. So I gathered a group of kids together that had been involved in gangs and violence. This group had never meditated beyond going to church before. I gathered them around me and I sat them all down in lotus position on the concrete. I began by telling them to close their eyes, and I taught them some of the teachings my father had taught me. I told them some stories that my grandmother had told me, and I gave them some teachings that I had learned in India. I finished off by repeating some of the beautiful mantras that I had learned in India. Pretty soon an hour had passed. I told them to open their eyes, and once they all had their eyes open, they began talking amongst each other about their experience. It was very funny because my drunk friend said to me, "Jose, what did you do to me? I'm not drunk anymore." I laughed and assured him that I hadn't done anything to him. He had been meditating for over an hour and had been able to clear his mind—not to mention that it was probably enough time for the alcohol level to drop in his system.

Every weekend after that when they would throw a party, they gave me an hour to speak to them and bring them into that place of meditation and peace. The beautiful thing was that when the neighborhood would go into gang–related conflict and violence, they would all protect me and send me home so that I would be safe. They called me the Barrio Buddha.

Everyone can feel that spirit, that truth that resides in all of us and is the same in all of us. This truth makes us all one and creates what we call *humanity*. If my friends—who were trapped in the barrio of Tijuana, a world infested with gangs, violence, alcohol, and drugs—could find it, I knew it could be found anywhere.

After my return home from India, I made myself an altar in my home. I had many different objects of power from all the different religions and spiritual practices I had already experienced in my life. I had some rosary beads from my Catholic background and a condor feather that was given to me by an Inca Shaman from Peru. I had a picture of Swami Kaleshwar and a statue of Shiva and Vishnu from the Hindu tradition. And I had a pair of dream protectors, sculptures from an African tribal belief system.

Each of these objects has different spiritual aspects, not only to me but also to the tradition from which they originated. A friend of mine from the Catholic tradition saw my altar and told me that it was a "giant contradiction" of what my spiritual practice "should be." I laughed and told him that my spiritual beliefs don't come from one place. To me, all these teachings are beautiful, and all of them are spiritual. I am who I am because of everything I have experienced, and my mind has been open to many different belief systems. I told him that I don't follow any one belief. They all follow me because they are all a part of me, part of what I carry around inside me. They are part of my truth.

When I was living in the Los Angeles area, I decided to start wearing the robes of the Indian tradition I had learned from. They were the traditional white Indian robes worn by the Hindu followers. One day I was in a large spiritual bookstore in the Los Angeles area, a very popular meeting place for the New Age community there. As I was shopping and looking at everything, many people came up and asked me questions about life. They asked me about spirituality and the Indian tradition. They were all nice and attentive to me and had great respect for my appearance and the teachings I had to offer. It was a beautiful experience, and I enjoyed sharing with them.

Just a few days later, I was in the same area of Los Angeles. However, I had just attended a rock concert the night before. I still had on my black leather pants, a black leather jacket, and a black concert T-shirt. My tall black boots were wrapped in metal spikes, and my long, dark hair was snarled and falling down over my shoulders. I walked past the same spiritual bookstore and remembered my experience from the week before.

I walked inside, anticipating what I might find, and began looking around. However, I did not get the same response that I had a few days before. Nobody asked me questions or showed any interest in me. The only person who showed an interest in me was the security guard, who began following me around the bookstore. I got many disapproving looks, and I felt so uncomfortable that I left, making a mental note: "Appearance does matter." I was the same person inside. I had felt the same spiritual feelings from the rock concert the night before that I had felt from the teachings of the swami in India. I came to the conclusion that there is practice, belief, spirituality, and perception everywhere, and that it's all different. Fear of what's different engenders judgment and disapproval of what we are not used to. If I had worn my Indian robes to the rock concert the night before, I would have probably gotten the same disapproving looks from the metalheads as I got from the people in the spiritual bookstore.

Respect, acceptance, and love are everywhere. If we can tap into those things that are inside of all of us, then we will lose the fear of the unknown and learn to accept life as it comes. We will learn to love what is different and learn from every form of spiritual practice. I used to think how boring the world would be if we all had the same beliefs and perspectives. Our differences make us interesting, and our differences make life interesting. When you look outside at a beautiful forest of trees, is it possible to point out the tree that is wrong? Just as every living tree belongs in the forest, every living human is beautiful and perfect in their truth and their perception and their spiritual belief.

CHILDREN OF THE SUN

Our nature is to be free
we create with our word
mother bears her children
and here we are now my love

you and me shine
like the sun
shining bright
like ripples of love

controlling our word
impeccably driving on
the highway of love
enjoying the ride

gratitude is in the review mirror
the source of love and we are
the source of love we are love
all of us are children of the sun

respect is in the review mirror
the source of love and we are
the source of love we are love
all of us are children of the sun

Welcoming Home the Love of My Life

*Once we feel freedom, it feels like an eagle has emerged from our chest.
And then we have a judgmental thought that is trying to put the eagle
back into its cage. Remember the eagle is not on parole—it's meant to be free
like you and me. —A thought I had in Teotihuacan, Mexico*

Blinking my eyes anxiously, I looked intently at the television, trying to focus my eyes in order to see one of my favorite movies, What Dreams May Come. I was unable to see it. In trying to focus, my eyesight seemed to be getting more and more blurry. Earlier that day I had gone to the dentist to get a root canal. Everything seemed to go smoothly, and I felt fine when I left the dentist and headed back to my home in Malibu. As I drove, I gazed up into the rearview mirror and noticed that everything was looking a little blurry. I blinked my eyes a few times and felt a twinge of pain behind my eyes. I made it home safely, told my wife that I wasn't feeling great, and went to lie down. I had the thought that if I slept, my eyes would get better and the pain would go away. When I awoke to the sound of the movie, I could see that my eyesight had gotten worse. I went out to where my wife was sitting and told her that I felt like my vision was getting worse. We quickly called the doctor and went to a clinic close by.

It was late on a Friday night, and the doctor said there was nothing they could do until Monday. Then we could go to UCLA and get some tests to see what was happening. My wife called my father, who was in New York doing an event. He told us to go directly to Tijuana, Mexico, to see my aunt, who is an eye doctor.

My wife drove me to Mexico as quickly as she could. As my aunt checked my eyes, she began dropping things. I thought to myself, *This does not sound good.* I asked her if she was going to be able to save my eyesight, and she replied, "I'm not concerned about saving your eyesight. I am concerned about your brain." She quickly called my uncle, who is a neurologist, and she drove me to the hospital he worked at. As he did the necessary tests, he found that when they had given me the anesthesia at the dentist, they had hit a nerve. It was affecting not only my eyesight but also my brain. He began pumping the medicine I needed into my system to reduce the swelling between my eyes and my brain. He said we could only wait to see if there had been any permanent damage.

As I lay in the hospital bed, everything was black. But because my eyesight was gone, all my other senses seemed to be heightened. All the thoughts in my mind seemed to be spinning out of control, and my negative self-talk seemed to be so much louder. At the same time, my mom and aunts were surrounding me with love, crying for me and praying that I would be okay. I could feel my ability to choose which thought to focus on and how my body would react to each, whether negative or positive. I found that if I focused on the negative thoughts, my body responded with a deep despair. I felt my heart close up and my muscles grow tense and anxious. However, if I changed the negative thought to a positive one, I was more apt to feel content. My heart opened up to those around me who were showing their love through their tears and worry for my well-being. I was then able to comfort them and help them know that I was okay. Eyesight or no eyesight, I would be fine with whatever happened.

I had been completely blind for five days. It took those five days for me to gain full awareness of my thoughts and figure out my ability to change them. It was constant practice, but being completely blind allowed me to practice any time I was awake. It was the only thing I had to do to entertain myself. I was tapped so deep into my inner self that I realized it was just that—a form of entertainment. It gave me the sense that my thoughts were not real. My thoughts are only my perception of what is going on around me and what is happening outside of me. My truth is what resides deep inside me. My truth doesn't change. It is always peaceful and full of love. My thoughts and perceptions, on the other hand, are what cause a reaction in my physical body and the way I feel about myself as a human. I have full control over those thoughts as long as I remain aware of what they are. Without my vision, I was able to really focus on hearing and on feeling my body. I was able to tap into that truth just a little more easily. Each one of our physical senses bring in outside stimuli, which feed the ego and add more and more stuff to our perception and our thought processes.

On the sixth day of being completely blind, I surrendered to the blindness. I had become fully aware of my other senses and began using them to become aware of my surroundings. I could feel when someone entered the room. I could hear my own inner voice much louder than usual, which made it easy to understand the emotions and feelings attached to that voice. Tasting became a wonderful form of pleasure, and I found a new understanding of enjoying a good meal. A hug or a touch from a loved one also became wonderful forms of pleasure, heightened due to my newfound ability to live completely in the moment of the touch. Because I couldn't see my visitors with my eyes, I became fully aware of who they were through hearing them and touching them. Most important, I began feeling, more than ever before, the spirit of love, the truth that is deep inside, and the pure understanding of what I am beyond my physical body, beyond my five senses.

That night I fell into a deep and restful sleep, and I began to dream. I dreamt I was in the desert and that there was a cave in the distance. I was walking hand in hand with my wife toward it.

As we got closer, I noticed there was a line of souls waiting to go into the cave. I had the feeling that whatever was in that cave was not what the souls really needed. I told my wife to take the souls and assist them in going to the sun. My wife left me and began directing the souls toward the sun as I made my way into the cave.

It was dark and cold inside. I went deeper and deeper, pining for what the souls had been searching for. Suddenly, a big demon appeared. His face was red, and his eyes were dark and shiny like onyx. He had big horns on each side of his head, and his hair was long and as black as the night. His stature seemed to mirror mine perfectly—short and stocky. He angrily said to me, "How dare you take the souls to the sun? They are the food I feed upon!"

I replied, "Those souls are not yours to feed upon. Those souls belong to the sun just as you and I do."

He laughed in my face, loud, maniacal, and mocking. His hot, fiery breath burned my cheeks as it blew through my own long dark hair. I closed my eyes in fear and let his laughter surround me, doing my best to not let my instinct to turn and run overcome my desire to help this pitiful creature. I thought to myself, *If I stay here and face this demon, the worst thing that can happen is that I could die and leave this physical body. But my spiritual body will only go home, where it is safe and infinite . . . just as it is here in this cave—safe and infinite.*

I opened my eyes, realizing the truth of my being and the illusion of what was happening outside of it. Just as I did, the demon jumped toward me and wrapped his large mouth around my neck, piercing my skin with his sharp fangs. I closed my eyes and knew it was the end of my physical body. I wrapped my arms around the demon and said to myself, "If it is the last thing I do, I will forgive this demon." I held him tight, and with all the love I could muster, I forgave him for his actions toward me and the spirits he was feeding upon. I opened my eyes, and I no longer saw the demon. Instead I saw myself as a little boy. I saw myself going through all the stages of my life, from a five-year-old to an eight-year-old to a twelve-year-old to a fifteen-year-old to a seventeen-year-old and finally to the age of twenty-four, which is the age I was at the time. I looked at myself and said,

"Thank you for coming back for me. All those souls that you sent to the sun—the ones that were waiting to enter the cave to feed the demon—were you. They were your future self." I awoke from the dream and realized I was still in the hospital.

I opened my eyes, and I could see just a little bit of light. This was the first time in seven days that I had seen anything other than complete darkness. Excited, I rolled out of the bed and covered my butt with the hospital gown. I felt my way to the bathroom and looked at myself in the mirror. I could see a very faint version of myself in the mirror. I looked at my physical being. I felt my body, and I heard my truth so fully and so peacefully that I knew I was going to get my eyesight back in full. I remembered my dream, and I told myself, "I forgive you. I forgive you for any pain you may have caused me." I knew at that moment that I was truly the love of my life. I could feel the fullness of the words from the brilliant master, "Forgive them, for they know not what they do."

"Forgive me, for I know not what I did," I said to myself. I forgave myself, and I understood that I have the power to make better choices in my life. I realized then that I was in charge of my own actions and reactions. I knew then that love does not come from anyone or anything outside of me. Love is inside of me. Respect is inside of me. Demons and pain are also inside of me, but the joy of forgiveness resides there as well.

If anyone outside of me attempts to hurt me, that is all it can be—an attempt. I have the power to choose how I react to that attempt. I can be like Buddha and turn the poisoned arrows into roses, or I can take what they say to heart and hurt myself with their poisonous words. With such powerful awareness, no one can make you feel guilty; you choose to feel guilty. No one can make you feel little or stupid; you choose to feel those things. You choose to hurt yourself with their words or actions, and you choose your reactions to them. My father said, "We are the only living creatures on this earth that punish ourselves a thousand times for the same mistake." We not only punish ourselves, but we punish others over and over again for the same mistake. When you or someone you love makes a mistake, allow the natural con— sequences to render, and then move on. There is no reason to continue to punish yourself or anyone else over and over again. There is no reason to hurt yourself over and over again. Make the changes and the choices in your life that will help you take care of yourself and continually move forward.

If someone has done something to you that was unthinkable or unforgivable—perhaps an act of abuse—allowing that action to ruin your life five or ten or twenty years later continues to give that negative person power. Take your power back. Forgive them not for their sake, but for your own sake. How can you enjoy your life if you are carrying around something negative that doesn't even belong to you? Do what you need to do to move forward—whatever that looks like to you.

Remember you are the love of your life. You create your own movie, which is the story of your life. When that movie becomes blurry and you can't clearly see where you are going, it's time to take action. It's time to take care of yourself, tap deep inside, and find that clear perception of who you truly are. No one else can take care of you the way you can. No one fully knows you the way you do, and no one can love you the way you can love yourself. Once your love for yourself is full and complete, it has nowhere to go but out, overflowing to everyone and everything around you. After all, you can only give what you already have, and it's all inside of you.

OUR ETERNAL KISS

I'm in love with nature
and love is creating free
the artist is creating its world
inside every imaginary mind

love is the key
to unlock the doors
that we locked
a long time ago

love is behind those doors
and those doors are made of love!!!!!!

shine bright like the sun
be who you are
an expression of love
a unique story from your heart

we are the pyramids
waking up from a long dream
and the dream remains the same
I'm still in love with you

you be you and I be me
together we'll sing
together we'll dance
romancing further than the infinite
or space and time beyond fear and dreams
you inspire me

I am you and you are me
you and me
together we'll sing
romancing our dream
in an eternal kiss

Supporting the Love
of My Life

Stop going against yourself by sacrificing yourself. Listen to your own voice and have the courage to live by it, creating a beautiful atmosphere for the love of your life. Begin this by serving yourself with unconditional love.
—Mama Gaya

I was sitting at the border of Mexico, waiting to pass over into the San Diego area and sweating profusely. I could smell the marijuana I had strategically stashed in the crotch of my pants.

I had been living in San Diego with my father for a few months now, removing myself from Tijuana and all the memories of my colorful past. That day I was missing my friends and the contacts I had become so comfortable with there. I decided to make a trip back to Tijuana for a visit. I asked my mother and my grandmother if they would like to come with me. They agreed, and once we were past the border into Mexico, I dropped my mother and grandmother off at the mall and headed off to see my friends.

I first went to see my dealer. I scored a couple of joints that I thought I could share with my friends in Tijuana before heading back to the States. However, I was unable to find any of my old friends, so I headed back to the mall to pick up my mom and grandma. I wasn't sure what to do with the joints I had scored, so I wrapped them up tightly in plastic wrap and hid them in my pants.

As we waited in the long line of cars waiting to pass the border, I heard the bark of dogs going from car to car, excited to do what they were trained to do: catch anyone with drugs trying to get into the United States. I didn't have much, so I naively thought that perhaps they wouldn't be able to smell it on me. The dogs suddenly came up to our car and barked profusely. They barked and barked until the Border Patrol came and made us all get out of the car. They detained us, including my mother and grandmother, and impounded our car. I willingly gave them what I had stashed and told them that it was only me. I asked them to please let my mother and grandmother go. I saw fear and confusion in my poor grandmother's eyes and heard my mother's loud, tearful words, "I never thought this would happen to me." I felt a giant, thick wave of guilt flow through me. It remained there like tar filling up a pothole.

After a few hours, they finally released my mother and grand—mother. As I watched them leave, I was relieved; however, the guilt remained. I vowed to never put my family in a situation like that ever again. They kept me detained for more than ten hours, which seemed at the time like ten days. I worried about my mother and grandmother, wondering if they were able to find a ride home. The Border Patrol questioned me over and over again, but because it was my first offense in the United States, they finally let me go. I paid a large sum of money to get my car out of impoundment, and I headed home to face the truth—the truth of my intense guilt, the truth of my lies, and the truth of the destructive mask I was still wearing.

My father was waiting at home for me, and in his hand he held a ticket with my name on it. It was a plane ticket to Egypt for the next week. He didn't say much about the incident at the border, but spending two weeks in Egypt with him on one of his intense journeys was punishment enough to me. His teachings at that time were very intense, and I, of course, was rebelling against them. Instead of fighting against the trip to Egypt, which was my first inclination, I decided to count my blessings. I took the ticket and thanked my father for allowing me to participate.

The trip to Egypt was one of intense learning. Because I was clean from using any substance, my mind began to clear. I was able to see myself in a different way. I decided I really wanted to change my life, and I began listening more to my heart rather than to my mind, which seemed to be telling me that I needed a substance. I met some of my father's apprentices, as I did on many of his trips. However, this time was different. I began to partici—pate amongst them and really listen and learn from them as well as from my father. I began to make friends, and I found one person in particular that seemed to reflect my desire to change my life.

Judy was a beautiful woman who was nineteen years my senior, but I was completely attracted to her inside and out. I first met her on the flight to Egypt. This was back when you were able to smoke on a plane, and due to the length of the flight, nearly everyone from the front of the plane had migrated to the back to have a smoke in the "smoking section." I was actually seated in that section and had migrated to the front of the plane to get away from all the commotion. I happened to sit next to Judy, and we began to talk. I was wearing a large pair of sunglasses that covered nearly half my face, and the first thing she did was lift my sun—glasses up and look into my eyes. She said, "Your eyes are just like your father's, and that makes me love you." We talked for a while, and she told me about an abusive relationship she was no longer in, a broken marriage, and how she had been saved by my father and his teachings. When everyone was migrating back to their seats, I stood up to head back to my seat in the smoking section. She said, "One thing I do know about myself is that I will never get married again." And as I walked back to my seat, I thought to myself, "I'm going to change that woman's mind."

I was twenty—one years old at the time we met. We spent every moment in Egypt together. My intention was to change my life, and falling in love seemed to be the ticket out of my unhealthy lifestyle. I was a virgin until then. I made love for the first time while cruising down the Nile River. With this new—found pleasure, my love for Judy grew even stronger. When we returned back to California, my grandmother expressed great disapproval of our relationship. However, I was so in love with her that there was no way I was going to listen. This was my ticket out of my crazy lifestyle. My grandmother, Mother Sarita, told Judy that if she was going to be with me, she needed to marry me. Sarita told Judy that I was just a child and that Judy needed to take care of me. So Judy, having great respect for my family and my grandmother, did just that. We were married the next February.

I moved to Malibu with Judy, and our relationship was great for the first year. We were perfect, clear reflections of one another, but it was very hard for me to see it through the smoke I had created. It clouded my vision of what was truly happening. Our unmet expectations of one another set in, and we stopped accepting each other. We both began to drink, and the ideal relationship that was supposed to change my life turned into one of manipulation and pain. I had so much guilt and pain from my past experiences that I could not allow anyone in, and she reflected me perfectly.

The abuse we had both experienced throughout our lives—abuse from others as well as our own self-abuse—was magnified in our attempt to form a loving relationship. There was no self-love in either of us, so neither of us had anything to give the other. What we did have to give were pasts full of manipulation, guilt, and pain. And those things came flowing from the both of us in full force. There were moments of love, but those moments were getting fewer and farther in between.

I had been taught what a relationship was supposed to be like through watching soap operas and listening to the chatter and gossip of the women in my life. Many voices from my past spoke up when thoughts of leaving came into my head: "You should never cheat on your wife or divorce her." "Marriage is forever, and you should stay with one woman." "You should never be like your Dad." Judy would start to cry if I ever expressed thoughts of leaving, and guilt would set in. I truly wanted to be the hero and the hopeless romantic that loved the same woman "until death do us part." But how could I love her when I didn't even know how to love myself?

I began eating too much and drinking too much. Eating was one of the ways I found pleasure, and drinking was an escape. I gained a lot of weight. I was very unhappy and unsatisfied with who I was and what I had become.

One day I was assisting my Grandmother Sarita in one of her classes. She did trainings and classes on healing, and I was her translator that day. The class had just ended and I was sitting in a corner of the room, watching as a little woman that appeared to be in her early fifties approached my grandmother. She said, "Mother Sarita, I think my husband is cheating on me, and I don't know what to do." My Grandmother replied, "I don't deal with those issues anymore—now go!" I looked at her with great surprise. I had never seen her be so firm with her students, and I thought to myself, *No, she didn't just do that.*

My grandmother looked right at me as I was having that thought and replied, "Yes, I did just do that, Son. Now come here. I did it for you. I waited until I was seventy years old before I finally realized how I was allowing thoughts like that to have power over me. I was seventy years old before I decided it was time to take my power back and not give any person or thought outside of me the power to control my own happiness and peace—my own self–love. You are young. It's time to take action and take your power back. Find your own self–love, your own self–respect and your own worth. It is not in anything or anyone outside of you, Son; it is all inside of you. Love and respect yourself enough to detach from an unhealthy relationship, and in return love and respect your partner enough to let her go." I knew exactly what my grandmother was talking about, but it took three years and my grandmother's passing before I mustered up the courage and the self–love to take action.

Judy and I separated from each other after nine years of mar–riage. When I approached her, she was defensive and hurt and didn't understand that I was coming from a place of peace and love. I knew that our relationship was toxic for both of us. To remain there was like feeding us both poison. It was difficult in the first year. Our poisonous habits continued to show up even after the separation. However, being outside of it helped me to see how poisonous it really was. I was able to enjoy time by myself and find the part of me that had been lost in a world I wasn't prepared for—a world that took me from one poisonous place and put me right in the middle of another, a perfect reflection of my addictive habits and my self–destruction.

After a year of taking care of my body and really finding myself, I was able to begin the true healing process. The process brought me to a place of pure truth, a place of self–love and self–respect. I began eating healthy foods, I stopped drinking completely, and I lost over fifty pounds. I was feeling so good about myself and so full of love that I felt perhaps I was ready to let it extend out. I started looking for a new relationship.

On one of my father's power journeys in Teotihuacan, I reunited with a beautiful woman that was close to my age. I had met her on many occasions, but because I was married, I didn't ever get to know her or become too close of friends with her. She had been studying with my father for a few years, and I thought for sure she would be a perfect fit for me. We both seemed to live the teachings of my father, and I thought, *What a wonderful opportunity for me to find a person, a Toltec teacher, that could teach alongside me!* I had taken a year off from teaching, and my first book was coming out in just a month. I was getting ready for a year of book touring.

We spent that trip in Teotihuacan flirting and getting to know each other. With a full heart and the excitement of being with someone new, I looked forward to the next time I would see her.

The next day we all went back home. She lived far away, but we kept in contact until we met again at the end of January on a cruise to the Mayan ruins. We truly hooked up then, and we eventually got engaged. Could this be the love I had been searching for? I really wanted to be a father, and I still felt that I wanted to be the hero and the hopeless romantic—the man that could stay with one woman until "death do us part." She seemed to be the perfect fit. She was beautiful and stylish; she looked like the girls I used to only dream about. She had a pretty good following of students and was a teacher of my tradition—what could be more perfect?

She came home with me from that trip, and after only a week, the poison started setting in. I began to notice my same old pat—terns and habits bubbling up. When she tried to change me, I responded quickly to keep the peace. To avoid feeling inadequate or guilty, and to make her happy, I made the changes she wanted. When she began screaming at me or crying for her way, I would quickly respond as if I was walking on eggshells again. I was afraid of losing this relationship; it was just such a perfect match. Then, one day, my ex—wife called. She was kind, and she thanked me for loving her enough to let her go. She said she had finally realized the poisonous cycle we were in, and she wanted me to know that she was happy and grateful.

Her phone call came at just the right moment. It gave me an awareness of what was happening. All my old relationship habits were coming back to the surface. I was losing myself in this woman just as I had in my past relationship. I decided to commu—nicate my feelings to my new love, and she began to cry. Enraged, she screamed at me, "If you really love me, you will eat my shit just like all my friends do! You will worship me just like all my old boyfriends do!" Guilt and shame and a desire to try and work things out began to bubble up inside me. I began to feel uncom—fortable. I took a deep breath and closed my eyes. I knew at that moment that she wasn't the one for me. Love for myself filled my heart and overflowed throughout my body, stifling out the old, habitual feelings of shame at trying to please someone outside of me, at trying to be the noble romantic and doing everything to make my woman happy.

I took her to the airport the next day. I felt a large sense of relief in knowing that I did the right thing. In the next few weeks I returned to my old self again, exercising, eating healthy, and doing things that I loved to do. I went to many concerts and started my book tour. I decided not to limit myself to one girl. I thought I would play the field for a while.

I met a few girls while traveling on my book tour and had fun exploring the dating world while continuing to learn more and more about myself. I was on a fast road to self—exploration, self—healing, self—acceptance, and forgiveness. In every relation—ship I got into, I lived by my father's words: "You are only in charge of your half of the relationship. You cannot be in charge of the other half." I put my focus on being in charge of my own happiness, my own self—love, and my own self—respect. I shied away from anyone who tried to put me in charge of their happiness, self—respect, or self—love. I could see the destruction in that thought process. When you put your happiness in someone else's hands, they will always let you down. It's too much pressure. I stopped trying to be the hopeless romantic hero who tried to make everyone happy. I found it so much easier and less stressful to be in charge of my own happiness. The best part was I could see the love and respect I got from others as well. It was almost impossible for others not to love and respect me when I was fully loving and respecting myself.

I was able to find a couple of different healthy, happy, and loving relationships. I was completely honest with my partners, and they were completely honest with me. Eventually I was able to fully commit to a beautiful, intelligent, and kind woman who was a perfect reflection of self—love and self—respect.

I learned in that process that love, respect, and even faith and spirituality are not things you find outside of yourself. It seems we are all searching for something outside of us to bring us happiness or faith or love, something outside of us to save us or bring us peace. In reality, these things are tucked away deep inside you, just waiting for the opportunity and approval to come out and shine. Once you find those wonderful things inside, you begin to fill yourself up with them. Love, respect, happiness, faith in yourself, all of those things that everyone seems to be searching for will fill you up and then extend out to everyone around you. When you love yourself, it's impossible for you to not find love. When you respect yourself, it's impossible for you to not find respect. You attract into your life a perfect reflection of what you are projecting from inside of yourself. When I look back on all my past relationships, it's so obvious. It's certainly an eye—opening way of looking at who you are.

What kind of people have you attracted into your life? If you are in an abusive relationship, look inside and see your own self—abuse. If you are in a healthy relationship, you are most likely balanced and happy. These projections have absolutely nothing to do with the person you are with—it has everything to do with you and how you perceive and treat yourself. "You attract into your life someone who abuses you just a little less than you abuse yourself"—a statement that brought profound awareness to my own life and the relationship I have with myself and, in turn, my relationships with others.

I am eternally grateful to my ex–wife Judy for her pure reflection and for the many life lessons I learned from her. My relationship with her taught me to love and respect myself. My relationship with her brought me to a place of peace and balance where I could attract into my life wonderful, happy, and healthy people.

Being in a healthy relationship has opened my eyes to the wonderful idea of being my own hero, my own savior. I never had to be that perfect, hopeless romantic that respected my woman so much that I vowed to never leave her. What I needed was to be the man who respected and loved myself enough that I could attract into my life someone that I would never want to leave, and that person is the love of my life. That person is me.

I am the only person I am always going to have. Everyone else is going to leave me in one way or another. To be a true hero is to be comfortable in your own skin, for no matter where you go, you will always be there. Instead of walking on eggshells trying to be there for everyone else, take care of yourself first, and all your other relationships will fall into place.

I look at life now as the universal honeymoon. I am on an eternal vacation with myself, and I want my vacation to be one that brings a smile to my face, a wonderful honeymoon that I will always remember.

GRANDMOTHER CROW

The elderly woman sings
and it is so contagious that you
sing along from your within
and to everyone you meet

and the crows continue
living their dream
living in a desert that no one will
ever know or see

they fly comfortably free
just to be the love of their lives
always letting free to be free

the old woman sings
what's important to you?
did you forget you're a crow
that got seduced by a parasite?

a dream of conditional love
the one that cut
its own wings to fly

and you make it alive
believing a lie
listen to your song
and set yourself free

remember your true nature
my beautiful child
mama loves its beautiful crow
so with unconditional love set yourself free

return home
wherever life goes

natural lover of life
natural lover of dreams

fly crow and spread your wings
and create a beautiful dream
the elderly woman sings

The Fallen Messenger

One hundred percent faith will guide you back home. —Mother Sarita

As I lay in the hospital emergency room, my stomach bleed-ing profusely from the gaping hole I had inflicted upon myself, my father standing beside me with tears streaming down his cheeks, I could not stop thinking about my best friend who had passed away six years earlier. I had vowed to him then that his death would not be in vain, that I was going to change my life and, in turn, make a difference in the world somehow. An intense amount of guilt and shame filled me for what I had just done to myself.

My friend was seventeen years old and full of life. I remem-bered some of the conversations we'd had together just before the weekend he was killed. He was talking about his hopes and dreams, knowing that he was going to create something cool for himself. He had his whole life ahead of him. Then, in an instant, it all ended. I thought of my selfishness and my strong desire to end the beautiful gift of life that had been given to me over and over again.

With that thought, my body began shaking profusely. I began convulsing. My father placed his hand on my forehead, and I

79

was able to look deep into his eyes. I saw a brilliant white light coming from my father's eyes and streaming into mine, and at that moment, everything went black. I passed out.

My life began flashing before my eyes. I was suddenly fifteen years old again, at one of the beaches in Tijuana with a group of my friends. We were drinking alcohol, and I became extremely drunk. My friends and I were standing on the rocks near the water, watching as the waves exploded on us every few minutes, showering water all over our bodies. Then one huge wave seemed to grab me and pull me into the water. I was being tossed around in the waves, doing everything I could to keep my head above the water. The current was so strong that it seemed to pull me down further and further under the surface. My body felt like a rag doll, and the ocean threw me around, beating me up as if it were angry at me. I struggled and struggled until I finally just gave up and relaxed my body. I felt myself sinking, and I knew I was drowning, so I began praying to the Mother Ocean. "If you let me go, I promise to spend my life serving others by doing what my family does."

At that moment, the waters calmed down, and my friend saw me floating on top of the water. He ran into the ocean, grabbed my body, and pulled me onto the beach. I began coughing and breathing deeply, so grateful for life at that moment, grateful for the second chance Mother Ocean had granted me. Not long after my fight with the ocean, I had forgotten the pact I had made when I got introduced to crystal meth.

I began experiencing memories of my life in the deep hell of drug addiction. I began pushing everyone away. My family and friends did everything they could to help me, but I continued to push them away. I lived in my bedroom, and my life consisted of being high, going through horrible withdrawals, and doing what I needed to do to score my next fix. The paranoia was so intense that I hid from everyone and everything. I spent days alone, ignoring everyone. I wouldn't eat or sleep. My mind raced with creative ideas, which added to the high that the drug provided.

The days turned into weeks and the weeks into months. It

all went by so quickly. I felt like I had no concept of time. I felt like I was unconscious but that every once in a while I would wake up briefly. In those moments I found myself in filthy abandoned homes, wondering how long I had been there. I was surrounded by people who felt like a swarm of bugs surrounding me and buzzing loudly, leeching and pining for something from me, something beyond what I could provide them.

I would wake up just enough to find myself in a dark, wet alley scoring my drug and paying a lord who was surrounded by men holding guns. The fear was intense and the paranoia was out of control. I found myself in parts of the barrio that I was told never to go in as a child. I witnessed crooked policemen and men that pretended to be policemen to take advantage of others, including me, both physically and sexually. The high was the only thing that stifled the intense pain of both the withdrawals and the dark, crazy life I woke up to.

I used any excuse to hurt myself in order to feel the pain that only the high of the crystal meth would take away. Doing the drug was the only thing on my mind and the only thing I cared about. I knew I could die at any moment living the life I was living, but to me that didn't seem to matter. I lived in this hell, thinking I was hiding it from my parents, until I was seventeen years old and my friend was killed in the accident. I knew that I could have been in that car. In fact, I knew that if it hadn't been for my father insisting that I spend the weekend with him, I would have been killed along with my friend and the others riding with him. This is when I made the vow to change my life.

I had been given yet another chance at living. Full of gratitude, I went to India to hopefully make a change.

In my dream, I saw myself after I had returned home from India. I had stayed away from drugs for a short time but soon fell back into the dark world of addiction. I was left alone in Tijuana. My family had all moved to America, and I chose to stay behind in my world of addiction. I was eighteen years old, and I had a home in Tijuana. This was the darkest point in my drug addiction. I hardly ever left my house. My home suddenly became one of those abandoned houses I used to wake up in. I woke up each morning finding other drug addicts sprawled around the house. I had provided a meth house for them to use in.

They brought me food and supplied me with my high as long as they could stay in my home. The people that had before seemed like bugs to me, surrounding me, buzzing and leeching, were suddenly the people I called friends. One day I decided to leave the house, and somehow I found myself incarcerated. I was in jail for a couple of days—long enough for my high to wear off and my thinking to become more clear. In pain, I hurried back to my home, hoping to find my next fix. I opened the door and saw the incredible mess I had made of my childhood home. There wasn't a soul in sight, and the filth was intense. My mind was clear enough to see what I had created, and it was dark and ugly. I had truly turned my world into a living hell. That was when I decided to turn my life around for good and move to San Diego with my family. Another chance at life. After that moment, I never touched crystal meth again. However, I kept myself in the world of addiction by using alcohol and marijuana.

My dream skipped me forward through my trip to Egypt and my unhealthy relationship with Judy. I now saw the huge fight Judy and I were in that very day, both drunk beyond con—sciousness and using terrible words and manipulation to hurt one another. I remember saying to myself, *Is this how you repay me for turning my life around? Is this how you repay me for wanting to change my life and start a family?* And, in slow motion, the event replayed itself in my mind. I walked to the kitchen and pulled a steak knife from the drawer. I violently stabbed myself in the stomach, not once but twice. I truly wanted to die this time. I felt there was no point in living anymore. Judy quickly called my father, and they rushed me to the emergency room. I was still alive.

As I lay on the operating table, I opened my eyes and saw a sheet over my head. My first thought was, *Am I dead?* But then I heard someone sneeze, and I said, "Salud." The doctor laughed and said, "Oh, you're awake." They had just finished stitching up my stab wound, and the doctor pronounced that I was going to be okay. I had yet another opportunity to truly live.

When I was rolled out of recovery and into my hospital room, my father was waiting there for me. He didn't say a word for a while; he just looked at me. I felt such remorse for my actions. I began apologizing to my father, and he asked, "Why did you do that, Son?"

I began to make up excuses for why I would stab myself. "I did it because you and Mom divorced. I did it because of the drug addiction. I did it because of Judy." I was relentlessly trying to blame it on something outside of me.

My father stopped me and said, "No, Son, you did it because you were stupid. Now hit yourself in the head."

I did as he said. Then he said, "Now do it again," and after a few hits, I stopped. I was tired of hitting myself. It hurt. My father said, "See? Now you are no longer stupid."

I then understood my responsibility for my own actions. There was no event, no other person, and no action to blame except myself and my own choices. Life again had given me another chance to really live, to really keep the promises I had made to the Mother Ocean and to my friend who had passed away so many years ago. And keeping those promises was my intention.

PAINTING

Painting I'm in love
creating with no judgment
I am becoming free, and it's perfect
the past has become nothing but ashes

angels have wings to fly
our imagination are the wings
only we can make our dreams
come true

what offerings did you bring?
what message did you give?
what's your message from within?
what kind of painting are you making?

and the message is simply you and me
creating a master piece of art
you and me
creating many masterpieces

The Four Keys of Transformation

Take responsibility for your actions, learn from them,
and use them to make a change. —Leo Ruiz

The four keys of transformation are the four key concepts I learned throughout my life experiences. These concepts assist me every day in remembering who I am and where I want my life to take me.

Now, let's imagine that you are in a relationship. You feel like everything is going great. You think you are happy. You believe yourself to be a caretaker, and you are in a relationship with someone who needs a lot of caretaking—a match made in heaven.

Suddenly, out of nowhere, your partner breaks up with you. It just isn't working for them anymore, and they want to start seeing other people. Heartbroken, you get your things and go back to your old apartment. You are feeling such heartbreak that you would do anything to numb the pain. You ponder drinking a big glass of wine or eating the entire tub of rocky road in the freezer. However, instead you remember that you are working on transforming your life, and you think of the first key to trans—formation: Acceptance—I will accept myself where I am today, without judgment.

You close your eyes and begin to breathe deep, allowing yourself to really feel the heartbreak you are experiencing. You put your focus on the pain deep within you, and you accept it in full, letting go of the urge to numb it with something outside of you. With the deep breaths, you are able to hear your heart beating and your body working in full unison with the universe. It is working for you without fail. Your heart is beating for you every second. It never stops. This thought resonates so deeply within you that the heartbreak you were experiencing before seems to be small compared to the vastness of the thought.

You realize that accepting yourself and life just as it is means allowing your partner to be just as they choose. You give up the idea of trying to control the relationship or trying to fix the relationship, and you come to a complete acceptance of what is. This brings peace inside your being, leading you to the love that resides deep inside you, the truth that we are all one and that we are no different from one another. This pure love is different from the kind of love you were practicing with your partner. What you were practicing was needy—I need to control you, I need to care for you. That kind of love is fleeting and false. True love encourages full acceptance, both of yourself and the life force around you.

When I was deep in the world of drug abuse, I had no awareness of my feelings. I was completely numb and oblivious to everything outside of me. When the high began to wear off, the pain was so excruciating that I was unable to accept it, which led me to my powerful addiction. Instead of accepting my life as it was and allowing it to be, I did everything I could to try and control it. Yes, I was just a young teenager, but I wanted to believe I had some form of control over my external circumstances. When this lack of control became apparent, instead of accepting it and allowing things to be, I numbed it with drugs and alcohol.

When my friend was killed in the car accident, it was the first time in my life I felt a good dose of my own lack of control. I understood then that there was something bigger out there that seemed to be controlling things. Something beyond the thick, scary mask I was wearing at the time. It was one of the first times

I was able to practice full acceptance—acceptance of who I was and what I was doing to myself and my life. Finally accepting and facing the consequences of my actions, I told my father how I was living my life. My journey to full acceptance began in India.

Once you are able to practice full acceptance—accepting reality the way it is and giving up trying to control things that are completely out of your control—you begin experiencing the next key to transforming your life: Honesty—becoming your authentic self.

Let's go back to the relationship and the breakup you just experienced. Once you were able to accept it, you realized that you weren't actually very happy in that relationship. You were pretending to be someone you weren't—the person you thought your partner wanted. You were wearing a mask. It was not authentic to who you truly are. However, you asked yourself at the time, "Who am I truly?" You begin to find that feeling deep inside again. You close your eyes, and you tap deep into your truth, beyond everything you thought you were and everything you were told when you were growing up. You see that you aren't really the caretaker you thought you were; that was just something you learned from your mother.

You remember how, when you were a child, you used to love to listen to music, play the guitar, and sing. You think about going to see some lighthouses and eat lobster on the East Coast. The thought excites you. When you get home, you book an East Coast lighthouse tour and pull out your old guitar and start strumming and singing.

Being honest about who you are means first being honest with yourself. Forget all the labels and the things you learned when you were growing up about who you were "supposed" to be. Start thinking about those things that felt good to you, what brought you joy or took you to a place where you were completely present.

When I married for the first time, I was looking for a way out of the dark world of drug addiction. Being so young, I thought getting married and having a family would be my ticket out. I removed one old, thick, scary mask, but instead of allowing my truth to come out, I replaced that old mask with a new one. I wore the mask of the noble hero, the committed husband and caretaker.

I had lost myself in a world of drugs at a young age, and then I lost myself even more in an unhealthy and abusive relationship. I listened to everyone around me to form what I thought should be my identity when in reality, my truth was still buried deep within, waiting for the moment I would set it free.

Once I was finally in a place where I could take a good, hard look at who I was pretending to be, I realized that it wasn't who I truly was. I stopped drinking and began taking care of myself physically. Not relying on food or a substance to bring me pleasure, I was able to slowly gain an understanding of who I was. This process is an ongoing one. It has turned into a fun and exciting exploration of finding the true Jose. Like I said before, I know what makes Jose happy, and I know what makes Jose suffer. How do I know this? Because I am Jose.

I listen to my truth more and more every day. I choose for myself those things that feel good from the inside out, instead of choosing things that feel good from the outside and hoping the inside will follow suit. In most cases in my life, it never has. When I am completely honest about who I truly am, a pure sense of peace resonates inside of me. I don't question my abilities or judge myself. Being honest makes it easy to fully accept myself and where I am taking myself in life. Like a beautiful master once said, "The truth will set you free." Be honest about who you are, and you will find your life transforming into a wonderful place of authenticity.

The third key to transforming your life is Discipline—taking responsibility for your own thoughts and actions.

Let's go back to the story of your breakup. It has been a month since your breakup, and you are browsing the local bookstore. You run into a mutual friend of you and your ex–partner's. He begins talking about your breakup, asking questions, and saying negative things about your ex. You begin to feel angry and hurt inside by the negative words coming from this friend. You start thinking your own negative thoughts, blaming your ex–partner for the breakup. Just as you start to verbalize your thoughts, you catch yourself.

You remember the positive changes you have made in your life and the acceptance and honesty you have found in the process.

Instead of expressing the negative feelings you were having, you tell your friend that the breakup was mutual and that you have only the utmost respect and love for your ex−partner. You say that you wish your ex−partner all the joy and happiness they can possibly find.

Surprised, your friend smiles and says, "Wow, you are doing great. You seem different. What are you doing with your life?" And the conversation changes into a much more positive and productive one. You begin sharing happy stories and ideas instead of gossiping about someone else.

When your friend leaves, you close your eyes and take a deep breath, still feeling remnants of hurt and negative feelings toward your ex−partner. You allow the feelings to flow in. You feel your heart beat, pumping blood through your body. You allow the feelings to be what they are, and you comprehend the amount of awareness you just experienced. The pure discipline you used to change the negative conversation into a positive one brought light into your own being as well as your friend's.

When I was lying blind in the hospital, I had the opportunity to become truly aware of the power of my thoughts and words as well as the strength of my actions. Because I couldn't see, my other senses became very strong. I began noticing that when I was alone in the room, fear would set in, and I would begin thinking about never being able to see again. I would start to feel anxious. My breathing would speed up, and my muscles would tighten. I also noticed that when my mother and aunts were in the room, I felt such love and gratitude for them that my fear would cease, my body would relax, and my soul would feel deep hope and peace.

I began practicing feeling different emotions just to feel the reaction of my physical body. I would think of a sad moment in my life and really feel that sadness. Then I would change that thought in an instant to something that made me laugh and feel joy. I began to notice that whatever I thought about, my body responded to, and it responded to each emotion in a different way. I realized that by changing my thoughts, I had the power to in turn change my physical reaction to whatever I was thinking—all in an instant. It took some discipline to do it, but when I got my eyesight back, I continued to practice. It was much harder with the extra visual stimuli, but I realized that I was responsible for my body and my thoughts, and therefore I was responsible for my reactions as well.

We are all responsible for where we are in our lives. If we are in an unhealthy relationship, we are responsible for being there, staying there, and attracting that into our lives. We are responsible for our actions *and* our reactions, and knowing this gives us power. It gives us the power to choose our own happiness, our own respect, and our own love.

Being able to master this discipline is a continual practice in my life. It's easier when I am in full awareness than when I am recklessly moving through life. Balance and focus is the key to mastering this powerful tool of transformation.

Last but not least is Respect—enjoying the mysteries of life.

Now imagine that you are still browsing the same local bookstore. You finished your conversation with your mutual friend, and you start looking through the books about the East Coast and the historical lighthouses you are about to visit. Suddenly you hear a familiar voice—the voice of your ex-partner.

You feel a little twinge of pain laced with excitement. You straighten your clothes and lick your lips as you turn the corner. You find your partner there with someone new, kissing and whispering in each others' ears. This is not the someone you were expecting at all; in fact, this someone is not even the same sex you were expecting. Your ex-partner has decided to live an alternative lifestyle. When the couple becomes aware of you, your ex becomes apologetic and embarrassed and tries to explain and make up an excuse. You walk forward and give your ex a warm, friendly hug and your congratulations on this newfound love.

Relieved, your ex introduces you to this new flame, and you respond politely with a warm smile. Your ex tells you that it's great to see you and tells you how radiant and happy you look. You reply likewise and you say you have to go. After hugs and good-byes, you walk away with a spring in your step. Your ex-partner's newfound love says, "What a beautiful person," as you remove yourself and head back to the joy of lighthouses.

When you are full of self—respect, you can't help but be respectful of others. Self—respect allows you to accept others just as they are because you accept yourself just as you are. You are able to enjoy the mysteries of life and the differences that reside in it. Different beliefs, different relationships, different personali— ties—you understand the magnitude of a life full of differences. Wouldn't life be boring if we were all the same? When you are full of respect for yourself, you don't have to change anyone else. You don't have to convert them to your beliefs or make them be someone they're not. You can allow them to be the person they want to be, and you can enjoy them fully!

It's like walking into an art museum and appreciating all the different beautiful styles of art. There may be some paintings that are your favorites, that speak to your soul, and some that don't. However, what if you walked into the art museum with your own paint supplies packed in your backpack, and when you saw a painting that didn't resonate with you, you took out your paints and brushes and start painting all over the paintings? Sounds ridiculous, doesn't it?

This is the same disrespect I see everywhere—people not liking other people's art, disapproving of their life's masterpiece and telling them they are wrong. Then they start taking out their own art supplies and forcing their life, their beliefs, and their style upon the beautiful masterpiece of a life that another had created.

So what does self—respect look like? Well, it's transforming your life into your own masterpiece of art. It's accepting your— self, your physical body, your mind, and being where you are. It's allowing your life to just flow.

When you judge yourself, you begin damning your growth and creative process. It's like swimming upstream, struggling to stay afloat while watching your life float by. Instead of being sad about what the river took away, flow with the river and allow everything that is your true, authentic self to flow along with you. Accepting yourself begets acceptance of others, which is one form of respect.

Be honest with yourself about who you are. Take the time to find your authentic truth. Who are you? What makes your eyes sparkle and your tummy tickle? What brings you the most joy in your life? Once you are honest with yourself, it's crucial to be honest with everyone around you. Respecting yourself involves taking off the many masks you wear and letting your true, authentic self shine out. This allows others to know who you truly are. You no longer need to fight and struggle to keep wearing a mask that is not really yours. Some will accept you and others won't, but if you respect and accept yourself, then what others say or do won't matter anymore.

Self—respect is having the discipline to take full responsibility for yourself and your life. Once you stop pointing fingers at others and blaming them for who and where you are, you begin seeing that you can make the changes in your life that will bring you to your truth. You will take your power back and begin to make the changes you need to make to respect yourself fully.

When I was sitting in the hospital with my gaping stab wound, I saw the pain in my father's eyes. I felt, inside of me, the disrespect I had shown myself through my selfish actions. With this self—disrespect, I also greatly disrespected my father and my family. It was the ultimate act of disrespect for the beautiful gift of my life.

It has taken me many years to even begin to master these four keys of transformation. I am constantly practicing accepting myself, being honest with myself, taking responsibility for myself, and respecting myself. But I do find that when I am fully practic—ing these four concepts, my life tends to fall into place. When I am feeling accepted, in charge of my life, and respected by those around me, I know these things are merely a reflection of me and who I believe I am in that moment.

THE ARTIST

An artist is painting on a canvas
a vessel of positivity
creating a message of love
for whomever has the time

slowly I notice that
wherever I go
I'm giving a message
I'm leaving footprints behind

sometimes I pretend not to see
not to be responsible
for the art I create
and I renounce that I know, until . . .

the questions are asked:
what am I creating?
what is my message?
what am I leaving behind?

I look in the mirror
to clear the smoke
to clearly see
and then . . .

I look into my own eyes
as they turn into an ocean
while I begin to sail away
into an empty ocean

in a vessel of love
I'm dreaming I am still the artist
that is dreaming of returning home
to you I understand now, I had to create my self first

I'm in someone else's creation
until the artist paints something to not be so empty
then I see the artist is me
then I begin to recreate after destroying
the dream of love

everything begins
to feel familiar as I set
my eyes to yours

feels like the first time
diving into your ocean of love
exploding into a rain of rose pedals
falling into our hands

so, what is your message?
where is your attention,
when you look at your reflection?
is the vessel of positivity leading you home?

Grateful
Awakening

Prepare by becoming aware of your life. Begin by noticing the things you want and the things you don't want. Make an act of power by making a decision from within, like planting a seed with love. Just like a movie direc-tor would say "action," take action to begin making a beautiful movie with gratitude and love. —don Jose Ruiz

With all my life experiences, I have started to see humanity and human life as I see nature. Let's use the example of a mature rose, vibrant with beautiful open petals. Suddenly a strong wind comes and blows the petals and the seeds of the rose into the air. The petals and the seeds fly around until they land in the mud, falling deep into the ground and the darkness of Mother Earth. The seeds remain there for a time, enjoying the warmth and love of the earth until one day they begin to feel the light of the sun. They feel the light and love and force of its true nature. The seeds get fed by the rains and the earth until they begin opening up. Suddenly, the seedling breaks out of the darkness and sees the light. It grows and extends its stem up toward the light, producing beautiful little buds and growing thorns to protect itself. Then the petals begin to open, spreading its aroma and beauty everywhere.

It's extending its love, its message of the truth of being a perfect rose. Knowing its fate, the flower detaches from its stem when it becomes mature. The winds come again and begin blowing the seeds around. And as they land in the mud, they feel the warmth of Mother Earth, and the story begins again.

This story reminds me of my journey. When I was a kid, I was just blossoming, feeling like I was moving toward the light. I began listening to everyone around me. Sitting in the ceremony, listening to the adults competing for the saddest story. My perception tempted me to find suffering, and I lost myself completely. But then I woke up, breaking the habit. It was a destructive song I didn't want to sing anymore.

In the Toltec tradition, there is nothing to learn except how to unlearn everything that takes our inspiration away. *Toltec* means *artist*, and we are all artists of life, creating our lives through our thoughts, perceptions, and actions. When we come into something negative, become addicted to suffering, feed upon those memories, or play out a part that is not our true self, it takes great discipline to let go of those memories, those feelings, or that suffering. With discipline in action, we get results.

One thing that helped me a lot was my father's book *The Four Agreements*. Every time I read it, it felt like the book had changed. I would hear a whole new message. My father would say, "The book didn't change; your point of view, your perception of life, is what has changed." I am grateful to the parents that I've had for doing their best and showing me unconditional love despite my choices, my addictions, and my manipulative behavior. Just like that good friend of mine, the rattlesnake. When it's young, it spreads its poison because it doesn't know how to control it. As it grows older, it learns to control its poison. I was young, just like the rattlesnake; I didn't control my poison because I was not aware of it. As I grew older, I became aware that I had poison and I was using that poison to hurt myself and others. Now, as an adult, I have learned to control my poison like the mature rattlesnake.

I truly believe in the religious idea of resurrection, but I believe it happens over and over again in this life. We get hurt or have a near-death experience or just decide we need to make a change. Every time we detach from something in this life, we are in the position to resurrect ourselves and make our life something new—just like the rattlesnake, who sheds his skin and moves on in life, enjoying his new skin. When I look at my past, I realize that I carried all my dead skin around with me. I continued to hold on to pain and suffering until I finally learned to let go and enjoy myself in my new skin.

There are moments throughout my day when I get a tickle in my brain. It reminds me of all the times I survived the crazy hells I put myself in. It makes me grateful to be alive. I still have all the memories, but I have learned to stop using them against myself and instead use them to remind myself of how precious life really is. I use them to remind myself that I am still alive and that I have each day to make my life one that I can be proud of. Each new day is an opportunity to explore my truth and become the person I would truly love to spend the rest of my life with.

I am eternally grateful for all my family and friends who helped me throughout my life and supported me in my quest to become a warrior. I am grateful to my spiritual guides, teachers, and masters who saw potential in me and thought enough of me to give me titles and positions of service where I helped others reach their greatest potential just as my teachers spend their lives doing. I accept those titles with deep gratitude and respect, but I don't see myself as a swami, a nagual, or the Eagle of the North. Those titles were given to me. I see myself as a kid from a bad neighborhood who gets another chance at life to serve and help others to find their truths. I cherish those titles with great respect, but when we believe in ourselves, we don't need a title—we are just grateful to be alive.

Remember the heart is always celebrating life because it is always beating. Take care of the love of your life and remember that you are here and have every opportunity to make your life a masterpiece of art.

About the Author

In 2010, don Jose Ruiz released his first book, *The Fifth Agreement*, in partnership with his father, don Miguel Ruiz. Following its publication, don Jose began traveling around the US, Mexico, and South America. Don Jose inspires people in many different ways, including book signings, lectures, seminars, and hosting journeys to Teotihuacan and other sacred sites around the world.

Among the highlights, don Jose has been asked to speak at conferences such as Conversations Among Masters, Celebrate Your Life, and the Conscious Life Expo. At these conferences, he has spoken alongside Dr. Wayne Dyer, Reverend Michael Beckwith, Caroline Myss, and Gregg Bradden. He has been interviewed by many notable media publications, including the *Los Angeles Times*, Univision, Fox News, and Eckhart Tolle Television. Don Jose has also inspired many corporate entities by using the five agreements to enhance positive rapport among employees and inspire creativity linked with common sense.

Don Jose's message has been heard all over the United States,

Mexico, Europe, Israel, Japan, and South America. His journeys to sacred sites have also been translated into many different lan-guages, including Spanish, French, and German.

Don Jose's message and *The Fifth Agreement* are growing rap-idly and being shared around the world. His message changes lives and brings people closer to themselves than ever before. His passion is to help children stay away from gangs and drugs by developing healthy outlets, such as music, as well as other creative avenues. He will continue to share the wisdom of his family lin-eage through his own life experiences. Don Jose enjoys working with people of all faiths and cultures. He sees all men and women as equals and feels it's a blessing to be alive.

DON'T MISS

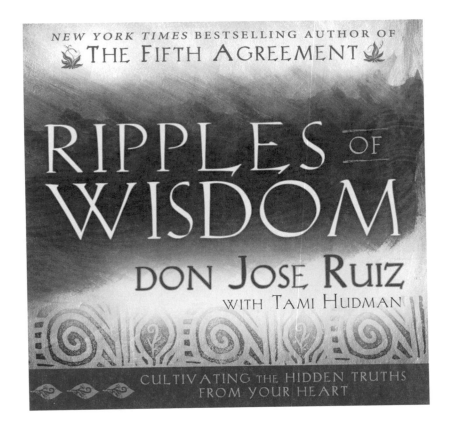

NEW YORK TIMES BESTSELLING AUTHOR OF
⚜ THE FIFTH AGREEMENT ⚜

RIPPLES OF
WISDOM

DON JOSE RUIZ
WITH TAMI HUDMAN

CULTIVATING THE HIDDEN TRUTHS
FROM YOUR HEART

NEW YORK TIMES BESTSELLING AUTHOR and awareness guru don Jose Ruiz teaches you to free yourself from self–deceit, fear, and conflict and live without limits in this collection of elevating pictures and quotes. The perfect gift for yourself or a loved one, this book combines ancient Toltec wisdom with new, practical insights to inspire a life of serenity and fulfillment. Open its pages and discover the hidden truths that will bring you closer to yourself and the world around you.